THE PHILOSOPHICAL APPROACH TO RELIGION

THE
PHILOSOPHICAL APPROACH TO RELIGION

By the same Author:

THE DAWN OF RELIGION
AN A B C OF PSYCHOLOGY
EVERYMAN AND CHRISTIANITY
THE PHILOSOPHY OF RELIGIOUS EXPERIENCE

The Philosophical Approach to Religion

BY

ERIC S. WATERHOUSE, M.A., D.D.

Professor of the Philosophy of Religion in the University of London

WIPF & STOCK · Eugene, Oregon

Wipf and Stock Publishers
199 W 8th Ave, Suite 3
Eugene, OR 97401

The Philosophical Approach to Religion
By Waterhouse, Eric S.
Copyright©1947 Methodist Publishing - Epworth Press
ISBN 13: 978-1-5326-3505-2
Publication date 6/16/2017
Previously published by Epworth Press, 1947

PREFACE TO THE FIRST EDITION

MY purpose has been to afford an outline of some of the fundamentals of the philosophical approach to religion for the general reader of theology, as well as for the students in my own College. That will be sufficient to explain the limitations of what I have written, in some degree at least, for I have desired to make the treatment sufficiently simple for the reader unversed in philosophy, whilst including the main problems of the subject. No one knows better than I do how such limitations afford material for the critical. I have left undone many things that should have been done, as well as done many things that should not have been done in an adequate, let alone an ideal, treatment of the subject. But if those who read will not expect more than my limits allow me to offer, realizing that simplification means omission of much that should be inserted, and an abbreviation of much else, as well as a certain false perspective in other ways, they will perhaps be kindly tolerant. Many statements that are disputable have necessarily been expressed summarily, without discussion, and thus may appear unfair to the side that does not accept them. Other subjects have been treated too briefly to envisage all the aspects of importance they possess. But this has been needful in order to keep the book within limits, and as there are a number of fuller and more adequate treatments of the subject available for all, it is to be hoped that those who want more will turn to them, for what I cannot offer, whilst those who want such an elementary treatment of the subject as this, will find here something towards their needs.

I should like to express my indebtedness to my son, Rev. J. W. Waterhouse, B.A., B.D., for reading the proofs, and making many valuable suggestions.

E. S. W.

RICHMOND COLLEGE
   SURREY
    June 1933

PREFACE TO THE SECOND EDITION

SINCE a second edition of this book has become necessary, I should have welcomed the opportunity of making a number of minor changes, such as most authors would desire to make in any book after it has been written a few years. This would have involved, however, in view of rising costs of production, a considerable increase in price. In the interests of students who use this book, I have decided not to take such a course. I must content myself, accordingly, with a few emendations of errors and obscurities which can be made here. On page 107, condensation of the argument has led to a sentence which has puzzled several readers. In line 35, the scent of the rose and the scratch of the thorn are referred to as 'brain-processes'. What should have been made clear is that what we call a sensation is a stimulus which arouses a brain-process and consequent perception. In common speech we refer to the scent of the rose as existing, whether or not we perceive it, wasting 'its sweetness on the desert air'. But we do not similarly think of the scratch of the thorn as existing apart from our feeling it. I was pointing out that this is not so; both are alike. The particles from the rose which touch the nasal membrane arouse a brain-process which we perceive as scent. The scratch of the thorn, similarly, arouses a brain-process which yields a sensation of pain. Neither sensation can be said in any intelligible sense to exist apart from the perceiving mind. I should also have made it more plain that it is possible to combine the idealist position in metaphysics with the realist position in the theory of knowledge.

E. S. W.

RICHMOND COLLEGE
SURREY
November 1938

CONTENTS

PREFACE 9

1. THE FACT OF RELIGION

   Religion's Origins—The Definition of Religion—The Relation of Religion to Human Life and Interests—Religion and Science—Religion and Philosophy—Religion and Art—Religion and Morality 13

2. THE PURPOSE OF PHILOSOPHY

   The Field of Philosophy—The Nature of Knowledge—Intuitionism—Empiricism—Pragmatism—Religious Knowledge—Scepticism and Agnosticism—Ancient Scepticism—Modern Scepticism or Agnosticism—Criticism of Agnosticism . . 38

3. THE IDEA OF GOD

   God and Human Reason—The Beginnings of Theism—The Growth of Christian Theism—The First Questionings—The Theistic Proofs—the Ontological Argument—the Cosmological Argument—The Teleological Argument—The Moral Argument—Belief in God as its own Guarantee—God's Nature and Attributes—Some Modern Quasi-Theisms 59

4. THE IDEA OF THE UNIVERSE

   Theistic Conceptions — Dualism — Philosophical Dualism — Monism — Monism and Religion — Pluralism — Materialism — Realism and Idealism 93

5. THE IDEA OF MAN

   The Moral Nature of Man—The Relation of the Individual to Society—The Personality and Freedom of Man 118

6. THE IDEA OF THE GOOD

   The Scope of Ethics—Theories of the Good—Pleasure as the Good—Perfection as the Good—Evolutionary Ethics—Ethical Intuitionism—The Basis of Moral Authority 131

7. GOD AND THE WORLD

   The Polytheistic Stage—The Pantheistic Conception—The Deistic Conception—Monotheistic Doctrines of God—The Idea of Creation—The Idea of Providence—Immanence and Transcendence 145

8. GOD AND MAN

   Reason and Revelation—The Conception of 'Natural Theology'—The Meaning of Revelation—The Function of Reason—The Relation of Reason and Revelation—The Relation of God to Humanity—Creation and Limitation—The Problem of Evil . 163

9. IMMORTALITY

   Early Beliefs—Later Development of the Idea of Immortality—Objections—The Arguments for Immortality—The Nature of Immortality 175

INDEX OF PROPER NAMES 187

Chapter I

The Fact of Religion

RELIGION'S ORIGINS

IN the middle years of the nineteenth century when the shock of the Darwinian doctrines was first felt, and a wave of triumphant materialism came as the backwash of that movement, it seemed to many that religion was amongst the superstitions exploded by 'science'. With the twentieth century came a swift reaction, and a recognition, such as had never previously entered man's mind, of the character of religion as a basic fact of human culture. Together with this, there came a newly-awakened empirical interest in religion, and a quest for the origin of a fact so inseparably woven in and through the history of human development. It had probably never occurred to any one of the Hebrew prophets to ask what was the origin of religion. In the story of Genesis, man begins with God, and the divine-human relation was never otherwise conceived. Nor did the pagan world concern itself with the rise of the gods. What was accepted *ubique et ab omnibus* was unquestioned, much in the same way as Greek logic accepted its universals from common knowledge as fully sufficient, and as Aristotle accepted happiness (eudaimonia) as the highest of all practical goods at which political science aims, since both the masses and the cultured classes agreed in calling the aim happiness, though they did not agree as to its nature. Religion was an accepted fact, and its origin aroused little curiosity. A few, like Petronius and Lucretius, went further, but they did not call on anything beyond fear to account for belief in the gods. With the coming of Christianity, it was accepted without question that religion arose out of revelation by God, although heathen religions were rather to be regarded as misrepresentations from the Evil One. There, for fifteen centuries, the matter rested. Then came the Reformation, but its immediate result was not to give liberty of thought, but rather to exchange the basis of authority in religion. Another century passed before there arose a man who may justly be called an epoch-maker, neither for the quality of his thought nor for the truth of his teaching, but because he was the first considerable thinker to make an independent approach, untouched by theological prepossessions, to the questions of life and character. Thomas Hobbes did not lack his own prepossessions, one of which was the curious persuasion that his philosophy was 'mathematical' in its principles. He left no disciples and much reproach as his memorial, but if a man be reckoned by the reactions his thought provokes, as well as the indirect influence it possesses, Hobbes deserves well of history. It was at least a century, and more nearly perhaps, two, before the colouring of Hobbes's opinions ceased to be noticeable amongst the philosophers whose views were diametrically opposed to his. Butler's admissions as to the place of reasonable self-love were a concession to Hobbes, much more than a necessity to his own position, and right down to Nietzsche the line of his thought reveals itself, like the faint trace of a grass-grown track over the Downs. Hobbes brought to the problem of the origin of religion his own unwelcome candour. 'And in these four things,' he wrote in *Leviathan*, 'Opinions of ghosts, Ignorance of second causes, Devotion towards what men fear, and taking of Things Casuall for Prognostiques, consisteth the Naturall seed of Religion.' Hume shows little advance on Hobbes: 'The first ideas of religion arose not from a contemplation of the works of Nature, but from a concern with regard to the events of life, and from the incessant hopes and fears which actuate the human mind.' Both Hume and Hobbes served at least to put the problem forward, even if they were little beyond the stage where Petronius left it, when he said fear first made gods in the earth. Hume was answered by Kant who shared the deist's notion of basing religion on morality. Hegel followed with the theory that identifies religion with philosophy, a theory which finds a supporter to-day in Croce, who, however has none of Hegel's reverence for religion, but dismisses it as an inferior form of philosophy. At the same time as Hegel, Schleiermacher was passionately affirming that religion was an autonomous activity of the human spirit, a feeling of absolute dependence, which provoked Hegel's well-known retort that in such case Schleiermacher's dog was more

The Fact of Religion

pious than his master. Within a generation of the death of Hegel and Schleiermacher, came the Darwinian theory, and with it the science of anthropology, which took over from philosophy the task of seeking the origins of religion, and found in Tylor's theory of animism the first answer to the question. Belief in spiritual beings was Tylor's 'minimum' definition of religion, but it proved too large a minimum none the less, for mere belief in spirits is far from marking out the differentia of religious behaviour. Spencer's view that religion arose from ancestor worship proved too narrow, for ancestor worship is not a world-wide phenomenon, and the term 'worship' in this sense is more than suspect of question-begging.

Far back as anthropology carries us, it yet stops considerably short of a period when we can say religion 'began'. Neanderthal man seems to have buried his dead ceremonially, with implements and weapons laid beside the body. Yet to this race belonged the skull found in 1856, which was considered so definitely sub-human that at first there was dispute whether it should be identified as the skull of an ape or an idiot! The origin of religion cannot be a matter of historical knowledge, but merely of conjecture. Yet there is no reason to think that such conjectures need be any less trustworthy than similar hypotheses with regard to the origin of species. There is considerable evidence that can be gathered, and whilst present-day primitive peoples are as ancient as we are in evolution, they still reveal psychological reactions and mechanisms that cannot be far removed from those of mankind in the earliest stages. Indeed, they are recognizably akin to those which we ourselves exhibit in modified forms, and the difference between our own mental level and theirs is not greater than that we may suppose to be between theirs and that of the earliest races of man. If, as I believe, the psychological mechanisms of savage and civilized peoples are at root the same, they are likely to represent mechanisms which pertain to the very nature of mankind.

The chief criticism one is inclined to pass upon the various theories which undertake to account for the origin of religion is that they are apt to start from the wrong side, from the characteristics of the external world, or from some social practice, as in the case of Spencer's suggestion regarding ancestor worship, or Durkheim's view that totemism supplied

The Philosophical Approach to Religion

the basis upon which religion developed. The old and crude view that fear made the gods at least has this merit, that it starts correctly by basing religion in the psychological nature of man, and not in his observation of the outer world or in tribal customs. To assign religion to fear simply is quite insufficient. Man fears ghosts, wild beasts and many other real and imaginary terrors, and takes action against these dangers, but such action is not that which he expresses in his religion. Man's main concern is to banish the cause of his fears, and the psychology of the unconscious shows how repression works in this direction. But he approaches his gods, and that alone is a sign that he has come to regard them with something more than mere fear. Awe, as Marett pointed out long ago, is, much more than fear, the essential religious attitude, and awe whilst it contains an element, sometimes a large element, of fear, holds within itself also wonder and a sense of self abasement. Mere fear tends to wear away with familiarity of the feared thing, or at any rate with the sense of protection, and even with the demand for definite action against the feared object. Death does not hold enough fear to prevent man from fighting and hunting. The African native faces the lion bravely enough with hopelessly inadequate spears, and the Indian shikari tracks down the wounded tiger with a gallantry that results from long experience with the danger. If man merely feared the gods, he would have found some way of repressing the fear, even if only by repressing the thought of the gods, or resorting to some device which would have seemed to have nullified their powers, as in the story of the coolies who were kept at work by their white overseer in his absence, by the simple expedient of removing his glass eye, and leaving it to watch them. At last one hit upon the idea of covering it with a cloth, whereupon the whole gang resumed their idleness. Similarly certain fetish-worshippers are said to cover the fetish, if they are about to do something of which they are ashamed, that it may not see the deed. There is fear enough in all the simpler religions, and at a casual glance, it seems that fear is father to faith, but the psychological nature of religious behaviour is not by any means fully explained by attributing it to fear. Westermarck, who thinks 'the old saying that religion was born of fear seems to hold true, in despite of recent assertions

The Fact of Religion

to the contrary', admits that adoration of the gods is also very prevalent, and elsewhere remarks that the objects of religious worship are mysterious, awe-inspiring, supernatural. He distinguishes these characteristics from mere fear by remarking that the horse fears the whip but does not shy at it. (*Early Beliefs and Their Social Influence*, pp. 7 and 23.) This would seem enough to discount the other statement regarding fear, since awe certainly is not psychologically the same as fear.

We may set aside therefore the crude notion that religion is the outcrop of 'sheer funk', and yet we must seek its ground in the nature of man before tracing the sources of belief in the gods to outward nature. More than anything else I think man's sense of insufficiency together with his lively apprehension of the uncanny, the awe-inspiring, or 'Numinous', affords us the ground upon which both magic and religion first grew. Modern savages do not call on magic to do for them what they are well able to do for themselves. They would not expect magic to build a canoe, gather food, or light a fire, but they might employ it to give success to the canoe, to make food plentiful, or secure that fire frightened their enemies. Magic is called upon to do that which lies without the range of normal powers, and in like manner, religion was an attempt on man's part to secure his relationship towards the awe-inspiring aspect of his surroundings. Feeling his need of help in situations beyond his wits to meet, man must have felt as we should feel if we were called on to deal with some dangerous machine charged with high power electricity of which we knew absolutely nothing. He had not advanced far enough, in the earlier stages of his existence, to make such a thing as a deliberate experiment. But he was fully aware of his helplessness to deal with things which he implicitly believed were affecting him. It is characteristic of the hopefulness that has been the mainstay of the progress of man, and of that insistent conativeness that made him keep on trying, that he did not give up the situation in despair. It is fortunate for the human race that agnosticism has never been the doctrine of primitive minds.

What, however, could he do? The only agencies known to him were those of living beings, and as animism, or its sequel, spiritism, shows, it was natural that man should think of the powers that surrounded him, not as persons—that came later

The Philosophical Approach to Religion

—but as powers that were to be treated in the personal, not the mechanical way of behaviour. A savage will treat a piece of wood purely mechanically, but let him suppose that a spirit is within it, or that it has properties that do not belong to an ordinary stick, and at once his behaviour towards it changes from the mechanical to the personal type.

At this point the attitude called 'supernaturalism' may well have played an important part. Animal psychology shows us that the familiar is never an object of any interest other than that of displaying towards it the accustomed behaviour; and if it calls for no such response, it evokes no interest whatsoever. The unfamiliar, however, is always a potent centre of interest the moment it attracts attention. There is every reason why it should be. No pattern of behaviour towards it is known. The pressing question is how to behave towards it; how will it behave on its part? One of my dogs, taken for the first time in an electric train, though familiar with steam-train journeys, leaped up every time the brake pump was felt vibrating through the coach, and eagerly sought under the seat, or sat cocking his ears with a puzzled expression. After several journeys, he ceased to notice it. Hunters know well how to use the curiosity of the wild creature for their own purposes. But it is not merely curiosity that enters into the animal's mind as regards the unknown. The higher animals show definite signs of being aware of the uncanny, and I have known gun-trained dogs who were abjectly miserable in a thunderstorm.

Man shares with the animals the interest in the unfamiliar, and the strained attention towards the unfamiliar that emotionally affects him. The uncontrollable nervousness that many people still show during a storm is suggestive of the apprehensions that the portentous and powerful aspects of Nature would arouse in early man's breast. One does not imagine that he wondered why the sun shone and the rain fell, but an eclipse of the sun, a flood, an earthquake or shower of meteors would certainly not pass unregarded. It is the attitude of strained attention and awe towards this side of man's experience, that is called 'supernaturalism', but as this suggests a distinction between a natural and supernatural order, which it is not necessary at this stage to presume, 'supernormalism' would be the better appellation. The madman is sacrosanct to most

The Fact of Religion

primitive races simply because he represents something towards which his neighbours do not know how to react, and the unfamiliar is always the potentially dangerous, to be left aside therefore with a certain awe. Since 'supernaturalism' in its degree is an attitude in which animals share, it must have been exhibited very early in human history. In itself it is not in any way religious, but it does suggest a basis upon which religion could arise.

It would seem, therefore, that the origins of religion are not to be sought in worship, either of Nature or of ancestors, nor in morality which in its earliest stages had probably no connexion with religion, but rather in man's sense of helplessness and of the awe-inspiring, or if one will, the uncanny, in the world around him, and his attempt to secure himself in his relationship with it. As against Sir James Frazer's view that magic came first, and religion began when its insufficiency was seen by 'deeper minds', it is probable that both ways of approach were tried. Man must have developed considerably before he began to differentiate the magical and the religious, seeing that even now most religions show signs of an imperfect apprehension of that difference. At the beginning, it is not to be thought that there was any clear idea of the being or beings responsible for the supernatural. Nor would the power be thought of as impersonal. The earliest stage would be purely the practical question how to act in face of the supernormal happenings. Such ideas as the Melanesian 'Mana' represent this power neither personally nor impersonally. Later, however, under the influence of animistic or spiritistic conceptions, the power came to be regarded as an agency that might in its degree be approached as man approached human agencies, and it is at this stage that we leave the sub-religious and arrive at what can be called the beginnings of religion. When once man came to think of a relationship between himself and the supernormal powers he found in his world, the first stages of religion are reached. The subsequent stages, even till now, concern merely the character of that power, and the development of man's relation with it. Animals share with man the sense of the abnormal, but their concern is purely that of adjusting themselves to it or avoiding it. Man's greater mental powers would not let him rest satisfied with this, and led him on to think of

The Philosophical Approach to Religion

the power and of his attitude towards it, and so to that which above all else has made man more than the cleverest of the animals, his religion.

THE DEFINITION OF RELIGION

NO definition of religion has ever been framed which touches its every aspect in life, and none has found even a considerable measure of general acceptance. The reason is that religion is so amazingly complex. It touches life on every side. Its manifestations range from the orgies of savages to Spinoza's 'intellectual love of God'. It is both individual and social. It intertwines at the lower stages with magic, at the higher with morality, and yet is identical with neither. It embraces belief and conduct, reason and emotion. It is enshrined in creed and custom, and yet lives independently of either in the heart. Its meaning to a man is not dependent upon what it is, so much as upon what he is. Under these circumstances, we must not expect an agreed definition, and yet we need not abandon the task in despair. We can see some of the various ways in which religion has been described or defined. That at least will show the manifold nature of the subject. We can also express the preference that is suggested by our own standpoint in the matter, and this will serve better than setting forth a formal definition.

We will begin by quoting three definitions which are entirely expressive of their authors. Hegel defined religion as 'the knowledge possessed by the finite mind of its nature as absolute mind'. Kant said, 'religion is (considered subjectively) the recognition of all our duties as divine commands'. F. W. H. Myers expressed the conviction that religion was 'the sane and normal response of the human spirit to all that we know of cosmic law'. If any one, even slightly acquainted with the positions of the three writers concerned, were asked to say to whom each of those definitions belonged, there would be no doubt whatsoever as to placing them correctly. It is perhaps putting the matter too strongly to say that the definition of religion is a matter of individual taste, but it certainly often is a matter of the writer's general position and thought.

Sometimes so entirely a personal impression of religion is

The Fact of Religion

offered, that in consequence what is said fails to characterize religion in the general sense at all. Matthew Arnold's famous declaration that religion was morality touched with emotion, and God, Something, an Eternal Power, not ourselves, that makes for righteousness, is quite inapplicable to the lower forms of religion, and not a true characterization of the higher. Whitehead's epigram that 'religion is what the individual does with his own solitariness' may apply to some more highly developed minds, but is not descriptive of religion as a whole. Ames, an American psychologist, went to the opposite extreme in simply equating the religious with the social. Primitive religion is social in the sense that its observance is primarily a matter of tribal rites, and the higher religions have often declared that he who loves God must love his brother also. But as Durkheim has conclusively shown, the difference between the profane and the sacred is sharply marked at all stages of culture, and even for primitive peoples, not all that is social is religious, either from their own or from our way of looking at the matter.

Definitions in terms of intellect, which regard religion as a naive or reasoned theory of the universe, stress an aspect that is secondary in religion. Herbert Spencer said that religion was 'an hypothesis supposed to render the universe comprehensible', and that its message was that 'all things are manifestations of a Power that transcends our knowledge ' (*First Principles*, pp. 43, 99). This ascribes to religion a purely intellectual function that is by no means its chief characteristic.

Definitions in terms of feeling come nearer to the heart of the matter. McTaggart (*Some Dogmas of Religion*, p. 3) says that religion is 'an emotion resting on a conviction of a harmony between ourselves and the universe at large'. In adding emotion to conviction, he goes a step nearer than Spencer, even though the idea of God does not enter. Yet religion is not simply an emotion. Psychologically it is true that emotion always tends to pass over to action, and it is that element which is neglected here.

Definitions in terms of volition and action do justice to this aspect, therefore, better than those couched in terms of feeling alone. Sir James Frazer's well-known definition of religion as a 'propitiation or conciliation of powers superior to man which

The Philosophical Approach to Religion

are believed to direct and control the course of nature and of human life' brings out, as he claims, the two elements theoretical and practical, and also helps to distinguish religion as a conciliatory attitude from magic which is coercive, for the true difference between religion and magic lies in the state of mind of those who practise them rather than in any intrinsic difference between the practices. But propitiation is not the most essential characteristic of religion, and the idea of propitiating God is absent from the teaching of Jesus. A definition that is not suited to the greatest of religions cannot be satisfactory as a general definition of all religion.

On this account, the definition of William James is preferable to that of Frazer. James says, in the widest possible sense man's religion is 'the belief that there is an unseen order and that our supreme good lies in harmoniously adjusting ourselves thereto' (*Varieties of Religious Experience*, p. 53). This does not so clearly distinguish religion from magic, unless we accept the expression 'harmoniously' as indicating a friendly relationship. It has the merit, however, of meeting both the higher and lower types of religion, but should stress more man's dependence on that order, if only to distinguish religion from spiritualism.

Others have defined religion in terms of the process of making sacred. Crawley says, 'Where the child plays, the adult prays, both actions are forms of one and the same physical necessity, which we know as play' (*Idea of the Soul*, p. 296). From this point of view, sacred ceremony is the essential feature of religion. It is the expression of imagery which characterizes religion and play alike. But it is not purposeless imagery. All is directed to the preservation and enlargement of life. Savages will spend long periods of time enacting sacred dances, dramas, and the like, not simply for the love of the thing, but because important, even vital issues, are thought to depend on its proper performance, and thereby the life and prosperity of the whole tribe hang. Similarly, Durkheim states that a religion is a unified system of beliefs and practices relative to sacred things, that is to say, things set apart and forbidden. Definitions of this type avoid the mention of God or gods in characterizing religion, a course which Durkheim expressly approves. The fatal objection to this course is that it is a case of 'Hamlet' without Hamlet. Historical forms of religion afford overwhelm-

The Fact of Religion

ing evidence that the idea of the gods is their common feature. To quote the anomalies of Buddhism against this is a small objection, which becomes less when it is realized how many gods have been imported into Buddhism in most Buddhist countries. Religion is concerned with making sacred, but it is the connexion with the gods which is the important point, for many forms of magic admirably fulfil Durkheim's idea of beliefs and practices regarding things set apart and forbidden.

Another class of definition relates to the aspect of religion in which it appears as a form of valuation, or of conserving values. It will be seen that this is akin to the last type of definition in that it omits reference to gods, and therefore comes under the same criticism. Man has always sought values, but not all values are properly to be called religious, and such as are, always have reference to a divine ground of value.

After all this, it is not surprising if we find it hard to suggest any one definition of religion as generally satisfactory. The Comparative Study of Religion has rendered all definitions in terms of intellect alone, unacceptable, but as regards the rest, one might almost say that any serves up to a point, but that it depends upon what point it is desired to emphasize, whether the definition is regarded as satisfactory or not.

The main difficulties are to embrace in one definition the earliest and latest stages of religion, to distinguish religion from spiritism, ancestor worship, and magic, and to settle which of the many aspects of religion is most essential to the connotation of the term.

In framing our definition, we should recognize that religion is a normal, characteristic, and universal form of human thought and conduct, possessing also specific features which distinguish it from any other form of behaviour. We should indicate that religion includes both belief and also practical activities designed to further what is believed. It also concerns values which man desires but cannot himself attain, yet hopes to secure by relationship with a power higher than himself. No single definition can include all this without being far too cumbrous, but it should include as many as possible of these characteristics.

A short definition given by Menzies has often been quoted, religion is 'the worship of higher powers from a sense of need'.

The Philosophical Approach to Religion

But worship is hardly the most central characteristic of religion, and some Eskimos, according to Rasmussen, have relationship with gods they do not worship. Moreover the sense of need seems to exclude the motive of gratitude, and the definition does not clearly distinguish religious worship from ancestor worship. Ira G. Howerth, an American writer, has suggested 'religion is the effective desire to be in the right relation to the Power manifesting itself in the universe'. It is needful to stress the word 'effective' to do justice to the practical aspect of religion and the word 'right' to distinguish religion and magic, but if this is done, the definition certainly covers much in small compass.

If what has been indicated in the criticisms of various types of definition in this chapter must be summed up in an experimental definition, it might be expressed as follows. Religion is man's attempt to supplement his felt insufficiency by allying himself with a higher order of being which he believes is manifest in the world and can be brought into sympathetic relationship with himself, if rightly approached.

THE RELATION OF RELIGION TO HUMAN LIFE AND INTERESTS

FROM the standpoint of history it is clear that man's intellectual and social development proceeded in close touch with his religion. Those who profess to see in religion only superstitions that have thwarted man's emancipation of spirit, find little support in history, despite facts upon which such a charge can be made with some truth. Incidents there are, but none the less the general issue is not much affected by them. Not only was religion closely linked with moral development, and the growth of human ideals, but it was also the nursery of most human arts and of culture generally. The earliest kings, according to Sir J. G. Frazer, were priest-kings rather than warriors. At any rate the priestly and kingly offices were often united, even to the time when Julius Caesar was Pontifex Maximus. The earliest law court was the shrine, sanctuary or temple, long before Samuel judged Israel in Ramah. The earliest medical service was that of the shaman, medicine man, witch-doctor, or whatever else he is called, and later, as the command, 'Show thyself to the priest' indicates, the priest was the sanitary inspector and

The Fact of Religion

medical officer of health. The beginnings of science, especially of astronomy, were in the studies of the priestly class, and indeed, education generally was their possession almost exclusively, and was imparted by them. The earliest philosophy was largely of a theological character, and if it did not seek to 'justify the ways of God to man', it certainly often sought to explain them. Romance found a cradle in the myth and the epic poem, and the commerce between earth and heaven was a favourite subject with both. The art of the cave-man seems best explicable as magico-religious. Later art found its inspiration largely in the temples, images, and shrines of the gods. Music developed in connexion with religious ceremony and worship, and even games are closely connected with religious festivals, the holy days that were holidays.

The cultural importance of religion has been a discovery of the past fifty years. To generations accustomed to identify religion with Christianity, and to write all other faiths down as heathen superstition, it was not evident that before Christianity, religion had played a great part in human development. Religion was held to have originated of course in primitive revelation of some kind, and the most that was claimed for non-Jewish forms, was the quite baseless notion of the deists and others that 'natural religion' imparted to man certain truths about morality and the like, which had become debased.

When the science of anthropology grew with amazing rapidity after the impetus given by Darwin's theories, it became possible to see that in religion, man found a way from the sense-life to a world beyond the senses. It matters not how crudely he misconceived the first glimpses he had of spiritual values. The important thing is that he came to be able to envisage them at all. The definition of man as the tool-using animal is about as misleading an attempt to characterize the differentia of the human race as it is possible for any one to make. It is spiritual apprehension that marks out man, and though such apprehension may be expressed in art, music, philosophy, and other ways than religion, it is historically true that in man's earlier stages of development, religion, even if often it were the magico-religious, afforded the sole avenue of apprehension of the world beyond the senses. Yet it is this more than anything else that has been the cause and measure of human mental

The Philosophical Approach to Religion

development, not only in what man discovered of spiritual things, but in the exercise that came to his mental powers by reason of the apprehension of an invisible order of reality. In this way there was opened up to mankind a new world, and in his exploration of that world, he who was once but the wisest of the brutes, became human. His body may have crossed the border line between zoology and anthropology long before, but it was not until his mind, by reason of spiritual apprehension, became truly human, that man was really man.

Religion and Science

It has already been said that history shows that in the earliest days of their development, religion and the beginnings of science were one within the culture of the tribe or nation concerned, and as for many centuries education was virtually the monopoly of the priestly castes, it could not be otherwise. Even in the greatest days of Greece, science and philosophical religious speculation went together as in the brotherhood or colony founded by Pythagoras at Crotona. In the Middle Ages such pioneers of science as Grossetète, Copernicus and Roger Bacon were monks, and the very revival of learning which began the separation of religion and science was led by the Church. It soon came to be evident that the theological dogmatism which dragooned Galileo was making a cleavage between reason and 'revelation', but in Protestant countries a sort of tacit compromise was reached in the seventeenth and eighteenth centuries which allotted the physical world to science and the spiritual to religion, and as such men as Kepler, Newton, and Faraday were earnest Christians, the compromise worked fairly well.

The first signs of conflict came with the geologists' estimation of the age of the earth, which ill accorded with Ussher's chronology; and the publication, in 1830, of Lyell's *Principles of Geology*, marked a new stage in the relationship of orthodox dogma and science. The work of the geologists was the necessary foundation for the hypothesis of the evolution of species, and when Darwin wrote *The Descent of Man*, he was furiously assailed as a veritable Man of Sin and Antichrist. The protagonists arrayed against him seemed more concerned for the dignity of the human species than for the Scriptures, and as a

The Fact of Religion

group of scientific materialists rushed to the support of Darwin and attacked religion on its own ground, it became almost axiomatic that science was in opposition to religion.

That period has passed, unlamented. To-day, with an increased knowledge of the limitations of both science and religion, there is little inclination on the part of either to seek matters of controversy. Science and religion represent different aspects of man's quest for reality, and in the true sense there can no more be a conflict between science and religion than between science and art. Scientifically, most artistic representations are false, and for that reason Plato made his detracting criticism of art. We realize that by reason of art representing in one way what science needs to represent in another, art opens a field closed to science. It is not otherwise with science and religion. What is taught in the name of religion, and equally what is taught in the name of science, may conflict, but between science and religion as such there cannot be any dispute. To quote Genesis against geology is nothing whatever to do with religion. It is simply to set opinions held on one ground with those held on another, and the fact that the one is a ground associated with certain religious teaching makes no difference to its correctness. In such a matter, the issue lies entirely with the weight of evidence, and the scientific account of the origin of the earth has long been accepted by all whose opinion is of value in such matters. But, for example, the view of human nature set forth in the Sermon on the Mount, is to be preferred to the alleged 'scientific' evidence that man is merely a tool-using animal, not because it is the view of Jesus, but because it is the view that is best supported by the facts. Whether, as in the one case, the view thus supported is that associated with science, or as in the other, with religion, makes no difference whatsoever to the real issue. Even, therefore, where there is a conflict between two views, that conflict is not properly to be called a conflict between science and religion, and when we speak of science and religion generally as activities of the human spirit, the notion of conflict between them is as foolish as to speak of the conflict between art and music.

It was once usual to distinguish between science as dealing with 'outer', and religion with 'inner', experience, but this distinction must not be too closely pressed. There was a time

The Philosophical Approach to Religion

when science was concerned only with that which had sense properties. Yet it became evident that to explain the world of the senses, it was necessary to transcend that world. It was still presumed, however, that the reality beyond the senses would have properties similar to those of sense phenomena. For example, ether was assumed as the medium through which light travelled. As far back as 1887, Michelson and Morley made their famous experiment to ascertain what might be likened to the 'back-wash' in the ether as the earth passed through it. The result was entirely negative. Fitzgerald and Lorenz suggested that there might be a contraction of bodies according to their movement through the ether, though of course such contraction could not be noted, as any measure used to define it would itself be similarly contracted. This, it was suggested, might explain the negative result of the Michelson-Morley experiment. The significance of all this was not merely in itself, but in the indication it afforded that science had come to the point when the properties of the world of the senses no longer served to illuminate, but only to confuse, its search, when it was needful to pass from physical to mathematical conceptions to describe the character of the reality it explored.

But apart from this, science deals in any case with a selected aspect of reality rather than reality as a whole. The scientific conception of its facts may be likened to a line drawing which excludes for simplicity's sake certain characteristics of the actual object. A blue print means enough to the engineer to enable him to understand the piece of machinery it represents, but it is far from being a picture of the actual machine as the eye sees it. In one sense the print tells much more than the actual picture, in another sense it tells much less.

Similarly physical science is concerned with what is, with fact taken apart from value. Religion deals with what is, but also with what the actual means, and with what should be. The task of science is to explain, that of religion to interpret. A mechanic might be able to explain the construction of a machine, showing the mechanism that made it work, and at the same time be totally unable to guess for what purpose it was employed, that is to say, able to explain its working, but not to interpret its meaning. So science explains the universe, but the interpretation of the universe, if there is one, is not a matter

The Fact of Religion

that science undertakes. That must be left to religion which studies the values of existence and deduces from them what it takes to be the meaning of existence. As Kant long ago saw, God, freedom and immortality are not facts that can be scientifically demonstrated.

The fields of science and religion, therefore, are sufficiently distinct to allow both full scope without interference with each other. The so-called opposition of science and religion comes from the notion that religion is identical with its dogmas, and that whatever is not capable of explanation on the lines of the accepted science of the time is a mere matter of opinion, without significance in the actual scheme of knowledge. Yet to point out the different spheres of science and religion does not imply that the two can be treated as wholly separate. We have had too long the dualism of the scientific and the religious, as if man's experience could thus be split into incommensurable halves. At present, we have not the requisite knowledge to enable us to adopt a truly synoptic view of experience, but when and in so far as that is possible, it will be found that the scientific and the religious quest of man will come closer together as we see life more broadly and more as a whole.

Religion and Philosophy

That religion is identical with philosophy, and that it has nothing whatever to do with it, are positions which have been, and are still, confidently maintained. Herrmann, for example, expressly said that it was a matter of indifference to the theologian as such, whether philosophy was deistic, theistic or pantheistic. Hegel, on the contrary, declared that the truth of religion was found in philosophy. In all cases of such diametrical opposition, it is likely to be found that the disputants attach different connotations to the common terms they employ, and that is certainly the case here.

The identification of religion with philosophy seems to arise from an imperfect comprehension of the psychological character of religion. Croce identifies religion and mythology, and mythology with primitive philosophy, a proceeding that ill accords either with anthropology, or with the empirical characteristics of religion. Yet on these assumptions he argues that religion is identical with philosophy and that philosophy is the

The Philosophical Approach to Religion

true religion. The religion that is not philosophy is an arbitrary attempt against truth, due to habits, feelings and individual passions.

The plausibility of the identification of religion with philosophy lies in the fact that every religion implies a view of God and the world. But because religion serves as a philosophy in many cases, it no more means the same thing as philosophy than does the sword used as a ploughshare become the same thing as a ploughshare. Philosophy lacks that personal relationship with the object of its search that is so utterly characteristic of religion. In religion, theory is subordinate to practice. In philosophy the theoretical element is uppermost. The key to success in philosophical understanding is intellectual, in religion it is spiritual.

If the account of the origin of religion which has been given here is in any way an approximation to the truth, it cannot be said that in its beginnings, religion was a form of inquiry as to the universe, though it may have very early been joined with such speculation as man was capable of undertaking as to the nature of the supernormal or numinous. But in its earliest stages, as in its later, religion was an attempt to establish something more than an understanding of the object that aroused the religious reactions. It was an attempt to enter into a harmonious relation therewith, and had a vital interest, as distinct from the intellectual interest, of philosophy.

To the ordinary man, as well as to many early peoples, religion serves the purpose of such philosophy as is needed, but that does not imply that religion arises for this purpose. Few mistakes are more common than the assumption that what serves some social purpose must have been created for that purpose. It may be granted that a hard and fast separation of the religious and the philosophical cannot be made, but none the less there is a distinction, pointed out above, between the personal attitude of religion towards the ground of reality manifested in the universe, and the impersonal attitude of philosophy. Every developed religion, and most primitive religions, will be found to have an accompanying philosophy, but no one can suggest that the philosophy of the writer of Ecclesiastes, and that of the writer of Job or of Deutero-Isaiah, are commensurate, nor that the Johannine philosophy is necessarily that of other Christian writers. But a far greater similarity will be found in the strictly religious side of these writings. Jonathan Edwards acknowledged the same scriptures as John Wesley, but the philosophy of the two was poles apart. There is no single philosophy that can be identified with the Christian faith, and it is unlikely that there ever will be any such.

Religion and Art

Of the relation of religion to art it is not necessary to say much. No ground of dispute exists between them. The Semitic religions, it is true, have been suspicious of artistic representation of human or animal figures; and alike for the Jewish temple and the Muhammadan mosque, only decorative art was permissible. Yet the command against graven images cannot have been as strictly interpreted as is sometimes thought, for in Solomon's temple were found representations of lions, oxen and cherubim, and the 'molten sea' was supported upon the figures of twelve oxen. It was a representation of the deity that was forbidden. The Greeks, on the other hand, with a high degree of anthropomorphic imagination, sculptured the figures of the gods, and interpreted mythological conceptions in art, as well as symbolizing ideals in concrete form.

That religion has constantly been the inspirer of art, and that art has often helped to the expression of religious feeling, suggests the inner connexion between the two. As soon as art reaches the stage when it is no longer a mere representation of its objects, and becomes an expression of its creator, it joins with religion in the attempt to find behind the thing seen, its significance and value. Because of what it suggests rather than what it represents, art joins with religion in opening the vision to the unseen. Like theology, art symbolies what it apprehends. One point of difference between art and religion lies in this, that whilst each is an avenue that leads from the sensible to the supersensible world, religion brings with it the sense of a personal relationship with things unseen, whilst art, without the religious sense, does not. It is a one way route from the world of sense, religion has an up and a down way. In art we are conscious of our own creativity, in religion of God's. Of course many an artist has such a sense in his art, but that is in so far as he is a religious man, not purely and simply as an artist.

Then also religion has necessarily a closer connexion with morality than has art. The motive matters more, whereas in art the product is more than the motive. A work of art is complete in itself. It conveys its own message whoever was its creator, whatever his views or motive in its creation, but a religious act depends upon the motive for its character.

Then, once more, the connexion between religion, truth and goodness is not of the same order as that of art. Plato objected to art on the ground that the work of art was a copy of a copy, a copy, that is, of the object which itself was a copy of the Platonic 'Idea'. Whilst that can no longer be an objection, it remains that art cannot be identified with truth, except in so far as art is an expression of personal feeling, and as such of true feeling. The beauty of art lies often in the idealization of the actual fact rather than in its actual expression. Nor is art meant necessarily to be a guide to conduct, or for the spiritual and moral edification of the beholder. Art that was deliberately untrue or immoral would fail as art, because the wrong never widens our experience, as what is right does. Yet art is no more committed to being deliberately true and good than to being the opposite. As Shelley said in the *'Defence of Poetry'*, 'A poet would do ill to embody his own conceptions of right and wrong, which are usually those of his time and place, in his poetical creations, which participate in neither. By this assumption of the inferior office of interpreting the effect, in which perhaps after all he might acquit himself but imperfectly, he would resign a glory in the participation in the cause.'

Religion, however, has a definite mission as regards truth and goodness, and whatever in religion is shown to fail in either respect cannot continue to maintain itself. Religion and art meet in the realm of values and symbols, they have close practical affinities, but it remains that they represent distinct spheres of human life.

Religion and Morality

It has been stated in the earlier part of this chapter that the origin of religion seems to have been in man's attempt to set up a relationship with the super-human order of whose existence he was convinced, that by so doing he might help himself in situations beyond his control. In that, there is nothing that we

The Fact of Religion

should call from our standpoint specifically moral, although we must remember that to primitive peoples, the distinctions we make between the social, moral and religious had little meaning, all being blended in the undifferentiated custom of the tribe. But at any rate, it would seem that, technically, religion has roots separate from morality, and for that reason definitions of religion that equate it with morals are unsuitable.

It may be true that the earliest form of moral conduct was compliance with the social requirements of the community, as distinct from self-regarding actions, but that does not mean, as some would persuade us, that morals are identical with social custom, for the essence of moral as distinct from prudential action, is the sense of obligation, apart from consequences, to do what is thought to be the right. That such a sense exists is undeniable, although it is hardly correct to assume that it witnesses to a divine law-giver whose fiat gives strength to conscience. It seems rather to be a development of that instinctive sense of compulsion which animals exhibit to do that which is the rule of the herd or pack. All creatures which live in a community manifest that sense of pack law, and penalties are often exacted from the creature who disobeys it.

Such instinctive action is neither absolute nor unerring, but in the main it makes for the social well-being and efficiency of the pack or group. Although there is some doubt as to the existence of a specific 'group instinct' and indeed the whole question of the use of the term instinct in psychology is more or less an open one, it remains that there are reactions exhibited, without prior training, amongst all creatures whose organization is social, and one presumes that man would share this sense, and that social instincts, or whatever else they may be called, are as needful to him as instincts concerning his individual existence. The psychological roots of morality seem to lie here, however much development was needful before these intuitive tendencies to act in certain ways, and to approve or condemn actions in others, framed themselves into a moral code.

It is equally certain, however, that (early in this development) the moral and the religious, as we view them, grew into an indissoluble unity. The story of Achan illustrates the point exactly. Achan reserved for himself part of the spoil which on that occasion was specially devoted to Jahveh the tribal god. On another occasion, he would have been entitled to his share of the same spoil, but in this instance the tribes had vowed all the spoil to the deity. Consequently the whole army suffers defeat in the next engagement. Achan is discovered, and he and all his family put to death, not because he took the spoil but because his action brought disaster on the others, by offending Jahveh. The relationship with the god was far too close to allow it to be assumed that it was unaffected by the actions of any individual. For such reasons, it is easy to see how morality as the early races conceived it, was a social matter, and how readily the moral code would come to be attributed to the will of, and enforced by the power of, the gods. Though it may be that in actual origin the moral and the religious were distinct, their inter-relation soon became close, yet even so, when we recollect how the Hebrew prophets thundered against a people devoutly religious and imperfectly moral, we shall not assume that religion and morals are the same thing.

In the West, our tendency is perhaps too closely to associate moral rules of the less important type with religion. In India, the holy man, being poor, has not the money for his railway fare, and is not above trying to evade payment. No one thinks the worse of him for that. In this country, we should at once suspect the genuineness of his religious profession under such circumstances. Yet, on the face of it, does such a transgression of public honesty really mean that a man can have no spiritual apprehension? We do not like to admit that those who transgress the edicts of society may have a deeper religious sense than some who scrupulously observe them, yet the attitude of Jesus towards publicans and sinners suggests that He did not take our ordinary notions on this subject. We are too ready to accept a kindly disposition and careful observance of moral rules and conventions as the essentials of religion.

The actual connexion between religion and morality lies much deeper than our expectation that he who appreciates spiritual values should respect social values. It lies in the fact that we believe the moral law to be objective, and if the universe is to be interpreted as naturalism or materialism interpret it,

The Fact of Religion

there will be found no basis for any objective moral law. The objective character of the moral law does not necessarily depend upon belief that it is the will of God, but it does depend on belief that it represents the fundamental law of reality, as for example the Hindu and Buddhist doctrine of karma is held to do.

It is impossible to do justice to our apprehension of moral law if we are to regard it as the consolidated voice of the ages behind us. True, we must respect the experience of the past, but the past as such has no authority over the present. The moral law represents the most absolute and inescapable law known to man. In Butler's famous words, if conscience had power equal to its authority, it would govern the world. Whatever we may take to be the manner in which the moral law has evolved, its power over us is not found in its history, but in its intrinsic character.

One may be in considerable agreement with the contention of such writers as Westermarck, who consider that the origin of moral judgements is emotional rather than rational, without drawing the conclusion which he reaches, that therefore morality is subjective. To say that in all instances the unselfish action is better than the selfish is as objective a judgement as can possibly be made. It makes no difference whether the origin of such a judgement is rational, or whether, like other such judgements, it springs from the intuitive tendency we have mentioned that approves and disapproves of actions, a tendency the herd and pack exhibit. An instinctive or semi-instinctive source lies behind all our activities, and colours all our judgements. The rightness or wrongness of an action is not to be identified merely with the pleasure or pain it gives to the agent or to others, though these factors must enter into our judgement of it. The objectivity of morality does not mean that our own moral judgements must be right, nor does it imply that they must be the work of reason, but rather that moral law is independent of subjective tastes or tribal rules just as much as are the physical facts of the universe. They belong to the constitution of Reality. They are an expression of things as they are. It is on this account that morality has been brought into inevitable connexion with the God or Power behind the universe, and regarded as being as much an expression of

Him as the universe is an expression of His creative activity.

The indecision of moralists upon the vital question of the authority of moral law, indicates how much, in practice, morality needs the authority of religion. If there were no religion, morality would remain. It is too deeply embedded in habit, in social authority, too necessary to communal life, to disappear like some requirement of etiquette disappears when it is no longer enforced. But it would certainly tend to be prudential rather than moral, to depend upon rewards and punishments allotted by social opinion, or at best upon the goodwill of the individual, for its support.

This is not to assert that the answer to the question Why should I do right? is that God wills it. That question is inadmissible, for it assumes that what is right should be done, not for its own sake, but for the sake of something else, and the man who cannot recognize the authority of the right, will not recognize the authority of God. But the question as to the ultimate nature of the right, why is right right, has historically found an answer only in the belief that it is the expression of the law of things as they are, the law of the Source of our being. In other words, the objective character of morality lies as Kant saw, in the nature of God. Belief in a righteous God brings morality into the very constitution of reality, as nothing else does. Apart from that, its basis must be in the constitution of society, and although many profess to see and require no other basis, it remains that the history of morality would have been utterly different apart from its connexion in the beliefs of mankind with the nature of God.

Whilst, therefore, on the one hand religion is not to be identified with moral conduct, and on the other, morality cannot be said to exist simply as a corollary of religion, it is true that in practice the connexion of the two has been so close that the most effective agent for promoting and maintaining moral conduct has been religious belief, and the elevation of religious conceptions has come again and yet again from moral advance, as the ethical ideals of the Hebrew prophets witness. To those who add a religious experience to their moral sense, it seems evident that what God hath joined no man can put asunder. If it be true that from the point of view of theory, religion and

The Fact of Religion

morals are autonomous activities, it remains that from the point of view of practice, the history of both would have to be entirely re-written, had it not been for the close fellowship in which throughout the ages they have been found in the development of all races.

Chapter II

The Purpose of Philosophy

THE FIELD OF PHILOSOPHY

It may seem strange to learn that at a recent joint session of the two foremost philosophical societies in the country, the Aristotelian Society and the Mind Association, a symposium was presented under the title, What is Philosophy? and the three prominent thinkers who took part agreed that, in view of the present position in philosophy, it was time that such a question was asked. Perhaps the best way to understand why there should be need to review the whole function of philosophy will be to see how the present position has arisen.

The Greeks defined philosophy almost as variably as we do. To Pythagoras is attributed the definition of philosophy as 'the knowledge of things human and divine'. 'Philosophy', said Plato, 'is a resembling of the deity in so far as that is competent to man.' Aristotle described it by its pre-eminence as 'the art of arts and the science of sciences'.

It became traditionally accepted, however, that philosophy was pre-eminently a matter of reason, 'the attainment of truth by the way of reason', as Ferrier put it. But with the nineteenth-century growth of the sciences, a new problem arose as to the relation of philosophy and science. Some, like G. H. Lewes, wished philosophy to become the co-ordination of the results of the different sciences, or, in Spencer's words, 'completely unified knowledge'.

The distinction between science and philosophy is, of course, comparatively recent. Newton was called a 'natural philosopher' in the speech of his day, and until recent times, psychology and ethics retained the old names, mental and moral philosophy. The term science has now come to denote more specialized study of certain definite aspects of experience with a view to their explanation. Philosophy, however, cannot be content to be simply a systematization of sciences, for science accepts definite limits in its function, wholly ignoring, in the

The Purpose of Philosophy

work of explanation, any attempt at interpretation, and omitting all references to values.

Science is selective therefore, whereas it is the business of philosophy to be comprehensive. The Greek 'sophia' out of which the term philosophy is framed, meant speculative wisdom, and that is in some part why the traditions of philosophy have been that reasoning is the function that belongs to it, and that the rational is a measure of the true. But modern psychology has shaken the idea that man is characteristically rational while the brutes act upon instinct. It has shown that his reason is not the impartial judicial proceeding that the Greeks would fain have believed. Biologically, man's intellect has been an instrument of his adaptation to environment, or of his adaptation of environment to himself, but the purposive character of thinking, and its connexion with human ends and values, is no longer to be denied. Pure reason is a figment. A certain amount of 'rationalization' enters into all reasoning except that which is entirely abstract, and removed altogether from concrete experience. It is on this account that philosophers have been forced to reconsider their function, for after all the barrenness of mere reasoning as well as the evidence of genetic psychology, proves that the task of philosophy can hardly be said to be simply that of giving a rational account of our experience and assuming that this is sufficient.

We have already said that philosophy is not to be identified with religion, but there is much to be said for the contention of Professor Macmurray that philosophy is theology, not dogmatic theology, or Christian theology, but theology as the Greeks understood it, an account of the whole of man's experience as embracing the human and divine. That is much more than a rational account of experience. It includes the realm of values as well as of fact. It sees in the spirit of religion and of art, interpretations of life. Such a philosophy will not merely explain; in its measure it will try to interpret. We explain by showing how the thing we explain, functions. We interpret when we say what is its function. Lotze's celebrated saying that what should be might prove to be the ground of what is, Kant's contention that God, freedom, and immortality were the central problems of philosophy, explain Professor Macmurray's words. If we are to speak of philosophy as a form of theology, we must use the term theology widely enough to include nontheistic types. Even McTaggart, who declared he saw no reason to suppose that God existed, adding characteristically that such a conclusion offered no evidence as to what did exist, afforded a philosophy that was, in the sense in which we are now using the term, a theology, as is evident to all who read his book.

Some Dogmas of Religion

As the term theology has another connotation in ordinary use, however, it is better to avoid it in a definition, and to speak of philosophy as the quest for a consistent and synoptic view of all the implications of human experience. That allows of values being regarded as due matter for philosophy, and sets the study in the central position the Greeks gave it, as man's effort to see life clearly and as a whole. What specialized forms of study we are to include in the word philosophy will depend upon the relative degree of independence some of them have now reached. Logic, which deals with the correctness of our thinking, is a science that is at the forecourt of philosophy. Psychology, once a branch of philosophy, is now reckoned an independent science, yet one that no philosopher can ignore. Metaphysics generally is held to include ontology, the science of being, and epistemology, the science of knowing. Axiology, or the science of value, is another study that might be included in the general conception of philosophy. Ethics, aesthetics, and the philosophy of religion are all in one sense branches of philosophy, though the former pair are independent sciences, and ethics has particularly close relations with sociology and psychology.

Philosophy therefore represents a group of studies rather than one special form of research, and whilst of those we have named, metaphysics is most closely connected with what is called philosophy in the narrower sense, all come within the range of thought in which philosophy moves. Moreover, recent developments call for increased understanding of mathematical questions on the part of the philosopher, whose attainments must indeed be encyclopaedic if he is to be acquainted with all the materials of his study.

The Purpose of Philosophy

THE NATURE OF KNOWLEDGE

KANT said that the three essential questions of metaphysics were, What can I know? What should I do? What may I hope? Metaphysics has seldom granted attention to the latter pair of questions, but the first finds its answer in the science of epistemology. The type of utter scepticism, known as Pyrrhonism, though Pyrrho probably deserved better of history than to have his name attached to it, answers by saying that we can know nothing whatever. The history of scepticism shows how impossible it has been to remain in this position. It is necessarily artificial, since to say we cannot know anything is to state that we at least know that we cannot know, in other words that knowledge is possible. If it be taken to mean that we do not know whether we can know or not know, it is an empty statement, and leaves us as free to pursue philosophy as are those who refuse to do so. We may ask, What is truth? but to say there is no such thing as truth is meaningless, for that very statement itself must be either true or false. If it is true, it contradicts itself, and if it is false, there is such a thing as truth. Moreover, as Descartes discovered, when, for the purpose of making an entirely fresh start, he determined to doubt everything, there remained the indubitable fact that he doubted. That is to say we cannot, by doubting, doubt the fact that we do doubt. Scepticism has always been purely theoretical. No man has ever consistently acted as if he knew nothing, and as Vaihinger and others have shown, there is a true philosophy of 'as if'.

The general question of scepticism will come under review presently and at the moment it will serve if we point out that the sceptics of classical times taught that since all opinions were equally true or untrue, the best course was to suspend judgements. It is clear that they were not warranted in saying this, as there is no reason on their premises to think suspension of judgement better than making judgements. Sceptics usually content themselves, therefore, with denying the possibility of a certain type of knowledge, or with hinting that knowledge is not in some ultimate and generally undefined sense, true. But that is not the point. All that we imply when we say that we can attain truth is that our knowledge is valid human know-

The Philosophical Approach to Religion

ledge. It may not be, for example, knowledge as God knows things. Whatever be our theory, in practice we all assume as much as this, and treat what is known as valid for us who know it.

The actual term knowledge is one that is used in several senses. It may mean the sum total of what is known to man, or what any individual knows, but more generally it denotes the familiarities that are gained through experience. Such knowledge may also be of several types. Leibniz, for example, divided knowledge as obscure, i.e. when we have a vague notion; and clear, i.e. when our ideas are definite. Clear knowledge, he added, may be confused or distinct. As far as words go, this seems paradoxical, but Leibniz meant that a notion can be quite definite, whilst we are unable to explain it. Finally, distinct knowledge further subdivides into adequate or inadequate, according as it is accurate and scientific, or not.

We cannot, however, approach the question of knowledge from this angle, for, since Darwin, it has become evident that knowledge is a matter that must be approached genetically, and as a social, not an individual, acquisition. Feeling is biologically prior to thought, and the beginnings of knowledge lie in a vague feeling-awareness. Higher up the scale comes perceptual awareness, and not till language develops can there be anything that is to be called conceptual thought. In our dream life we revert generally to the primitive, and the mentality of most of our dreams reveals to us what is probably nearly akin to the more primitive forms of knowing. Our dog knows us, we say. He does so chiefly by scent. If the odour of our body and the tone of our voice changed instantly as we were with him, he would probably cease to recognize us, but he would not show wonder, as we should, if any friend of ours was transformed before our eyes. He would simply refuse to react to our commands any longer. In a dream, we descend closely to his level. We are speaking with someone, when suddenly that person changes to another. We are not surprised. We simply go on in our dream with whatever practical reactions seem necessary. That indicates the immediate, unreasoning, practical character of knowledge in its earliest stages, which despite all that supervenes in the development of knowledge, is never wholly lost,

The Purpose of Philosophy

Epistemology may be a branch of metaphysics, but no epistemology can proceed without a basis in psychology.

We cannot stay to trace the history of epistemological speculation. In brief, it may be said that it has alternated between rationalism and empiricism. Rationalism goes back to the Platonic 'Ideas', which Plato held we had known in the pre-earthly state, and so we recognize their earthly copies. Knowledge therefore was a form of recollection. Descartes, Spinoza, and Leibniz were all at one in regarding knowledge as belonging to the mind, and not, as empiricism held, impressed upon the mind from the outer world. The ordinary man, at first thoughts, naturally follows the empiricist. He is convinced that what he sees is there to be seen and makes itself seen by him. But after a little reflection, he may realize that when, for example, he sees a tree, the tree does not enter his mind, but what does happen is some process in the grey matter of his brain, and the relation between a process in the grey matter, the idea that somehow accompanies it, and the tree, is by no means simple. He may thus come to see how the rationalist and the empiricist took opposite sides, the one stressing the inner action of the mind, the other the outer world. Kant's critical philosophy occupied a mediating position in the theory of knowledge. He showed the falsity of Locke's celebrated notion of the mind as 'tabula rasa', a blank tablet, by stressing the fact that the mind is active in perception, and pointing out that there are certain principles of thought, relations of identity, difference, space, time, and so forth, that cannot be said to be given by experience, but rather are necessary presuppositions of the forms experience takes.

Kant's list of categories is now obsolete, but it remains that he was right in showing that the mind receives its impressions in virtue of its own inner activities, and that the forms under which we perceive do not belong to the objects perceived, but to the perceiving mind. The doctrine of evolution, however, raised an issue that Kant was not in a position to appreciate. For example, a human being who had never seen a square or a circle would presumably distinguish them at first sight, and perceive the equality of the sides of the square. We should be doubtful whether one of the lower animals would be capable of making such a distinction, and whilst an ape might learn to distinguish the square from the circle, it would not, one imagines, be capable of understanding the equality of the sides of the square. At what point, therefore, in mental evolution did things like this, which are self-evident to us, arise? Biologists warn us against accepting the notion that they could have been gradually acquired by previous generations and transmitted to the descendants. We may raise the question but we cannot settle it. If, as Dr. F. C. S. Schiller argued in one of his earlier essays, our axioms are merely successful postulates; even so, the origin of these postulates remains unknown.

The evolutionary theory, whilst throwing us back to the genetic method of treating the problem of knowledge, has not solved the problem, but served merely to clear the ground of some obsolete notions. For example, there was the old notion of innate ideas, that is to say the ideas which were supposed to have been implanted in the mind of the first man, and therefore were assumed to be latent in his descendants. It does not seem evident that any thinker of repute held the doctrine in the extreme forms which are now sometimes made objects of ridicule. There can be no innate ideas, but minds at any rate do possess certain pattern reactions, or common ways of reacting to the same situations. Were it not so, there could hardly be the practical similarity of experience that characterizes social life. But perhaps we had better turn to a closer consideration of one or two of the views of knowledge that have been, and are, current in philosophy.

INTUITIONISM OR INTUITIONALISM

WHAT has just been said naturally introduces the theory known as intuitionism or intuitionalism, a theory which has been more closely associated with moral and religious issues than with strictly philosophical questions, and has had close affinities with mysticism. In common to its many forms lies the fact that all have stressed the part played in knowledge by that which is directly and immediately apprehended. They have held that our apprehension of the right and the true is not due to a long process of tribal and racial development, but is immediate. The older types of intuitionism defeated themselves by knowing too much about intuitions. Lists of intuitively apprehended prin-

The Purpose of Philosophy

ciples were drawn up, tables of springs of action that instantly revealed the moral rank of our motives, and so forth. But that need not blind us to the fact that what is intuitive does play an important part in life and knowledge. Bergson is fond of insisting that we grasp life never by reason, but only through intuition. Reasoning may review what is past, or anticipate what is to come, but the actual present living moment of experience is grasped at first hand only by intuition. Dr. G. E. Moore adopts a kind of intuitionist position in ethics when he insists that 'good' is as indefinable as 'yellow', that is to say, it is an immediate experience, not a characterization of experience that can be explained by reference to something else. The mental side of instinctive activity is also intuitive in character, as animal mentality abundantly illustrates. Our difficulty in assigning the place of intuition in knowledge lies in the fact that about intuitions, as about tastes, there can be no argument. Yet it remains that knowledge cannot be limited to that which can be rationally expressed and explained. Its basis is undemonstrable, and some of its deepest certainties, the things for which men are willing to die, lie beyond the boundaries of what can be reasoned, but deep within that which makes itself undeniably known to us as true.

Empiricism

All who lay stress on experience come within the connotation of the term empiricist. It denotes an attitude rather than a school of thought. In one sense it is as old as the Greeks, but usually it serves to describe the line of thought that ran very diversely through Locke, Hume, Mill, Lewes, and Spencer, who with all their differences, such as Mill's individual and Lewes's cosmic experience, unite in regarding experience as the fundamental reality, and sense-experience as some kind of a mirror which indicates the actual properties of an external world. The attitude of physical science is strongly empiricist, for physical science takes the world as a fact, without reference to its apprehension by our minds, but this of course is a practical, not a theoretic, empiricism.

The old empiricism which regarded the mind as a kind of sensitised plate upon which nature impressed herself, collapsed in face of the fact that the mind is active, not passive, in sense perception. It perceives, as we have said, under categories of its own, which cannot have been 'got out' of nature, since until they are possessed, they cannot be seen in nature, for example the idea of causality; since as Hume showed, what nature actually presents to our mind is succession rather than causation. Similarly, what nature actually reveals is multiplicity of a bewildering kind, certainly not that unity which we postulate of her ways, yet never fully see. The waves that give us the sensation of light may act upon a plant, but do not make it see. The waves are the same to man and plant, the difference is in them, not in the waves. As Green put it (*Prolegomena to Ethics*, p. 47): 'A sensation can only form an object of experience in being determined by an intelligent subject, which distinguishes it from itself, and contemplates it in relation to other sensations.'

The mind cannot be a register of external reality which simply records what is given to it. We can arrange notes or colours in a scale, yet the notes and colours do not arrange themselves. Their arrangement is the work of the mind.

James laid stress on empiricism of a new type, which he called radical empiricism for these reasons. 'I say empiricism, because it is contented to regard its most assured conclusions concerning matters of fact as hypotheses liable to modification in the course of future experience, and I say radical because it treats the doctrine of monism itself as a hypothesis and unlike so much of the halfway empiricism that is current under the name of positivism or agnosticism or scientific naturalism, it does not dogmatically affirm monism as something with which experience has got to square' (*Will to Believe*, pp. 7, 8). James's empiricism was a philosophic attitude rather than a doctrine. He regarded it as the opposite of rationalism. Rationalism emphasizes universals and makes wholes of parts. Empiricism lays stress on parts, treating the whole as a collection, and the universal as an abstraction. It is a 'mosaic philosophy', a 'philosophy of plural facts' eschewing such universals as substance, absolute mind, and the like. It differs from the older type of empiricism, which was a doctrine of 'mental atoms', in that it holds that 'the relations between things, conjunctive as well as disjunctive, are just as much matters of direct particular experience, neither more nor less so than the things them-

The Purpose of Philosophy

selves'. As compared with pragmatism, James said that radical empiricism was not vitally different as a method, but none the less was an independent doctrine, an epistemology and a metaphysic which might or might not be joined with pragmatism. Its basis was that 'the parts of experience hold together from next to next by relations which are themselves parts of experience. The directly apprehended universe needs in short no extraneous trans-empirical connective support, but possesses in its own right a concatenated or continuous structure.' The older empiricism laid stress on the external world, and Kant on the connective principles of experience. James solved the difficulty in a wholesale fashion, to his own satisfaction at least, by assuming that both the external world and the connecting principles of thought were alike matters of direct experience, an attitude too summary to prove in the long run satisfactory.

Pragmatism

A modern way of approaching the question of knowledge is afforded by pragmatism, a theory which was received with considerable animosity by many British thinkers. It is possible that its awkward name, and the American origin and characteristically American expression of the theory, caused some prejudice in minds trained on the older academic lines, for pragmatism does not appear as objectionable as its critics would have us believe, if it is approached without prejudice. The term was coined by Charles Sanders Pierce in 1878, but it was left to William James and John Dewey to give full exposition to the pragmatist position, whilst F. C. S. Schiller vigorously advocated, under the name humanism, similar views in this country.

Primarily, pragmatism is a method or calculus, intended to be applied to metaphysical problems, rather than a philosophy. Its origin seems to lie in the reaction against mere reasoning which arose when the post-Darwinian genetic psychology demonstrated the fact that reason was to be considered as functional rather than judicial, a means of adaptation to environment, primarily applied to the problem of living rather than the power of abstract thought. Pierce declared that the meaning of any idea was developed by the consequences it was fitted to produce, and that our conception of any object was

The Philosophical Approach to Religion

determined by its effects. Hence practice was the criterion of life and reason alike, and on this account the name pragmatism (pragma, a thing) was suggested.

In one sense the pragmatic method is as old as philosophy. Socrates, Aristotle, Locke, Berkeley, and Hume all utilized it in some way. Pragmatism is clearly a form of empiricism, and its method was described by James as 'the attitude of looking away from first things, principles, categories, supposed necessities, and of looking towards last things, fruits, consequences, facts'. Papini described it as a corridor leading to many rooms. All pragmatists use the same corridor, but they arrive at different destinations by its means. It is even possible for a pragmatist to accept the doctrine of the Absolute, but instead of regarding the Absolute as the logical ultimate in philosophy, he will judge it solely by the practical consequences it may possess.

The central doctrine of pragmatism is its notion of truth. According to what has been called the correspondence theory of truth, ideas are true if they correspond to reality. Plausible as this appears at first glance, it is evident that it necessitates our assuming that we can know reality apart from our ideas of it and compare it with those ideas to see if the two correspond. This is manifestly impossible, since if we have any knowledge of reality at all, it can be only through our ideas of it. Philosophy has therefore been more inclined to what has been called the coherence theory, which asserts that true ideas are those which are consistent and harmonious amongst themselves. It is much in this way that we judge when we accept evidence from several witnesses, according as their independent stories form a coherent and non-contradictory whole. Yet it follows that only the whole of truth can be absolutely self-consistent, and therefore certainly cannot be reached short of omniscience, or the Absolute. Mr. Joachim, in *The Nature of Truth*, after a careful and critical examination of the theories of truth, came to the conclusion that no theory of truth as coherence could be completely true for it must be 'other' than the truth 'about' which it is. It thus fails in that concrete coherence which is complete truth, but none the less it carries us further than any other.

Such a confession opens the way for a hearing of the pragmatist view of truth, despite the fact that Mr. Joachim called it not a theory but the denial of truth. Pragmatism holds that

The Purpose of Philosophy

truth is not a logical characteristic of ideas, but a value, something that happens to ideas. They are validated by their practical use. Critics have professed to see in this statement the naked assertion that whatever works is true, a position that could not be maintained by any sane person. Pragmatism is not to be set aside so simply. It maintains that truth is validated only in so far as it is tested by the widest possible criteria, and that these include intellectual and aesthetic usefulness, usefulness in theory as well as in practice. Ideas which are parts of experience, are true in so far, and only in so far, as they put us into satisfactory relation, in the widest possible sense, with the rest of experience. On such a ground, we accept to-day the theory of relativity whereas it was on the same ground that formerly the conceptions of 'classical' physics were held to be true. The relativity theory explains certain facts better, yet it is likely that it will be subject to future modification in the light of fresh facts. The facts are the criterion, and yet facts have meaning only in relation to our apprehension of them. It would follow that we cannot concern ourselves with the notion of any absolute truth that bears no relation to our apprehension, but solely with truth as we can receive it.

Pragmatism therefore holds that we make truth, and also that we make reality. It admits a basis that we do not make, which is the condition of that we do make, but denies that we discover a complete and perfect reality by our intellect. That is a legacy of the Platonic 'Ideas'. It is our own experience that is creative of the reality we know, in its commerce with the ground of reality from which all proceeds. The character of the pragmatic method forbids that any one set of conclusions, realistic or idealistic, should result from its use. If the criterion of that which 'works' is to be accepted, no avenue that leads to results can be forbidden beforehand. Time and results will decide what will hold as true. At the cost of abandoning the hope of absolute truth, pragmatism at any rate has made the notion of relative truth much more forcible. It avoids the assumption that mankind is always doomed to live without truth, which is what we must admit if only the whole is actually the true. Moreover it eases the problem that must at times rear its head when we reflect that most of the theories of former generations are now not accepted as true. Have the greater part of the ideas of man-

The Philosophical Approach to Religion

kind then been false, and if so, how many of our own ideas are likely to be true for the generations to come? Pragmatism replies that a doctrine may be true for one generation, because it fulfils the needs for which it was set forth, but these needs are not unchanging, and as they change, the doctrine no longer works. It has not therefore become false, necessarily, but represents an obsolete form of truth. For example, the belief that the world was fixed in space represented a truth as long as it worked, and satisfied the needs which led to its formulation. Later it ceased to function, in view of fresh facts, and became untrue to those facts, although it was still true for the facts that originally were explained by it. The truths of one age are superseded just as the windmill has been superseded by the steam mill. Yet if we were back at the conditions of the former age, the windmill would still have its place and use. So would the truth that, like the windmill, has been left behind by the developing needs of the age. In the setting of its age it is still true, but that setting has passed, and hence the truth that was is not the truth that is. The value of this conception to our idea of religious truth is obvious, and those who are willing to accept the limitation that pragmatism puts upon the possibility of our knowledge of truth at least gain this much compensation, that thereby they are allowed to hold that no form which enshrines a true experience is false, though it will, as do all things human, become changed and inadequate with the passing of time.

Religious Knowledge

The weakness of the older theories of knowledge was that they were exclusively metaphysical. The psychological aspect was ignored, for psychology was virtually non-existent, and hence theories of knowledge lacked a sound basis. The theory of knowledge must go beyond psychology, but it cannot start elsewhere. Only by ignoring the psychological aspect of the matter has it been possible to advance the idea, once popular, that religious knowledge was a matter of faith or opinion, whilst scientific knowledge was a matter of fact. We have seen that knowledge in its ordinary meaning signifies the familiarity gained by experience. Such familiarity is truly knowledge, and therefore religious knowledge cannot be separated from other types of knowledge or classed as faith in contrast to knowledge.

The Purpose of Philosophy

All knowledge requires faith as a basis, faith that we can know, faith in the regularity of nature which is the assumption that underlies all our knowledge concerning its ways. Every scientific hypothesis is put forth in faith, and everything demonstrated based on that which must be accepted without demonstration. Only when we have agreed to our postulates can we demonstrate anything.

It may be said that whilst this is true, it is not in this sense that faith enters into religion, but in an additional sense. Some knowledge is demonstrable to all who can understand it, such, for example, as mathematical knowledge, whilst the ordinary knowledge of sense-experience is not disputed by any one. On the other hand, religious knowledge is personal and variable, and lacks demonstration.

This may be at once admitted, but it will be well to see why it is so. The certainty of mathematical knowledge lies in its abstractness. If we accept the premises, the abstract conclusion follows from them. But whilst the expression 'two and two make four' is a stock phrase to describe an obvious certainty, certainty is not the same as reality. It is absolutely certain on Euclidean geometry that two parallel lines cannot meet, but we are told that space does not conform to Euclidean ideas and owing to the 'curve' in space, of which we have heard so much of latter years, parallel lines may meet. It is absolutely certain by the first law of motion that a moving body in the absence of resistance will continue for ever, but that certainty can never be translated into experience. The certainties of mathematics belong to an ideal, not the actual, world. Similarly as regards sense experience. It will be found that the greatest unanimity lies in the reactions we have towards those things that are vitally important in the literal sense—important to the preservation of life. If our sensations of pain were as subjective as our tastes, we should soon perish. Nature takes care that the things that are vitally most important are pleasant, and those that are vitally harmful, painful. But where we come to things of less importance she allows us as wide a range as our tastes reveal. There is no commonly agreed 'fact' in that side of nature. Yet personally one may be as sure that one dislikes the sharp 'bite' of mustard as much as the scald of boiling water, and if every one reacted to mustard as to boiling water, we should be sure that mustard was as universally and objectively painful as we think boiling water to be. Yet this very sentence is significant in its inaccuracy. We transfer to the object the reaction it provokes in us, the scald we say is painful, the mustard hot. This indicates that what we think to be objective fact concerning sense experience is really objectified subjective reactions, and we have no scruple in taking this course when there is virtual unanimity about our reactions, but where, as in the case of tastes, they differ, we are not so sure they are to be regarded as certainty. In other words, certainty here depends solely on the overwhelming majority vote of experients. But a majority is not always an indication of what is true or real.

From the very nature of the case, we do not expect that knowledge of God will be found comparable with the common familiarities that come through our senses. All the ultimate points of our quests, whether those quests be scientific, aesthetic, moral, philosophical, just as much as religious, are mysteries, and those who seek them cannot find the common body of accepted fact that exists in the lower spheres of the senses. What is the nature of physical reality after all is ultimately just as much a mystery as the nature of spiritual reality. When we reach this sphere of thought, we find ourselves dealing with hypotheses rather than with accepted facts, and the notion that there is any more certainty as regards ultimate scientific truth than there is as regards ultimate religious truth, is baseless.

There is no reason, then, to differentiate religious knowledge as knowledge of any different type. It is knowledge of the same kind as any other, but its affinities are with our knowledge of the beautiful rather than our knowledge of the properties of objects of sense. We can scarcely compare the knowledge of nature possessed by Wordsworth with that of Darwin, but it would be sheer pedantry that denied to Wordsworth 'knowledge' of nature, because his knowledge was not of the type that can be inductively demonstrated. It has often been disputed whether the knowledge of God is intuitive or inferential. We may put it in a sentence by saying that knowledge of God is intuitive, knowledge about God inferred. The inferences we make about God may be as disputable as our theory of beauty, but the intuition of God is as personal and decisive to those who experience it as is the sense of beauty. No man can prove that the

The Purpose of Philosophy

beautiful thing he sees is beautiful, but he doubts not at all that it is. So with knowledge of God. It is immediate, a matter of insight, but when we pass from personal certainties to philosophical views of religion, we pass to inferences which, however strongly supported, lack the immediate certainty of the facts of inner personal experience.

SCEPTICISM AND AGNOSTICISM

WE cannot pass away from the subject of the purpose of philosophy in general and of religious philosophy in particular, without some discussion of scepticism that denies the possibility of knowledge, and agnosticism that denies the possibility of religious knowledge. The understanding of the latter begins in that of the former.

Ancient Scepticism

Scepticism is not a philosophy so much as the denial of the possibility of philosophy. It may be a philosophical method. Lord Balfour, for example, defended the place of philosophic doubt in thinking, but, as a permanent attitude, scepticism represents the despair of a philosophy of life. Yet in one sense it is as old as philosophy, for when once man began to think systematically he was introduced to the incalculable difficulties of such thought, and hence we find, long before the Greek sceptical schools, a vein of scepticism in Chinese and Indian thought, and in the attitude of Gotama to transcendental knowledge. The scepticism of Ecclesiastes may have been influenced by Greek thought, but it is thoroughly Hebrew in its attitude to life. Pyrrho of Elis (c. 360–270 B.C.), who was possibly a contemporary of the writer of Ecclesiastes, is generally reckoned as the first philosophical sceptic. He held that knowledge of the ultimate nature of things was unattainable. Hence suspension of judgement was advised, to secure 'ataraxia' or calm. All opinions were simply conventional, and were arrived at fortuitously. There was no necessary truth, and of any pair of contradictories, each was as true or as false as the other. The whole was a matter of indifference. Pyrrho was a representative of the reaction that came when the high expectations aroused by early philosophy were disappointed. He left no writings, and it is doubtful whether his teaching justifies the expression Pyrrhonism, often used as synonymous for utter scepticism. His real quest was practical, for 'eudaimonia' or happiness. He ridiculed human testimony, showed the untrustworthiness of the senses, the varieties of opinion on all subjects, and the dependence of our ideas upon convention. He concluded that this showed we really knew nothing and had better admit the fact. This line of argument was carried on by the Middle Academy of Arcesilaus (315-241 B.C.) and Carneades (214-129 B.C.). Arcesilaus maintained that his teaching was implicit in that of his great predecessor, Plato, and carried on a vigorous polemic against the ideas of Zeno and the Stoics. 'We know nothing, not even this itself, that we know nothing,' he said. His suggestion was that we follow the more probable in ethical matters as leading to 'eudaimonia'. Carneades, in a manner that reminds us of F. H. Bradley, attacked the Stoic theology and physics, pointing out the contradictions in the idea of God as both finite and infinite, universal and individual. He gave a doctrine of probability in three degrees. An idea was probable (a) in itself, (b) among similar ideas, and (c) in the most widely tested system of ideas. Yet this was directed toward a knowledge of the good rather than knowledge in general, and this school of sceptics seemed more concerned to ask 'Who will show us any good?' rather than 'How can we know the truth?'

The last phase of ancient scepticism came with the school of Aenesidemus, Agrippa and Sextus Empiricus. This later scepticism disowned the Middle Academy, a fact that does not alter the debt to it. Sextus laid stress upon the diversity of opinion on all subjects as indicating that no such thing as certainty was possible, and on the fact that all proof depended upon what had been previously demonstrated, and so led back to an endless regress. The writings of Sextus afford a full account of the school and indicate the state of intellectual bankruptcy in the age. In a manner that might be called Shavian, Sextus turns sceptical criteria upon scepticism and shows how absurd it is. His practical conclusion is that one might as well live according to custom, because it saves trouble. But one does not need a philosophy or even a criticism of philosophy to tell one to live according to custom. By this time, however, the tide of Greek thought was ebbing fast, and the rising tide from Galilee was carrying men's thought toward a new age of faith.

The Purpose of Philosophy

Scepticism was submerged. Even when the first days of belief were over, and scepticism raised its head once more, there was no sceptical philosophy, for the Church had by this time gained control and for over a thousand years maintained its hold, until after the Renaissance and Reformation, learning, especially in Protestant lands, shook itself free, and philosophy was able both to think and to doubt for itself.

Modern Scepticism or Agnosticism

Hume, who called himself a theist, because he admitted (whether or no he believed it) that faith might establish beliefs that have no rational basis, was more than any one else responsible for reviving scepticism. Kant said Hume woke him from his 'dogmatic slumber', though Kant's scepticism was as regards the power of pure reason to give knowledge of God, freedom and immortality, which, he held, were given by 'practical reason', The term agnosticism was due to Huxley, and referred rather to doubt as to our powers of solving ultimate problems than to religious scepticism, which is what the term now suggests. Spencer also defined it in this sense, as the attitude which held that 'ultimate scientific ideas are all representative of realities that cannot be comprehended'. Hence Spencer called God the Unknowable. Because any doubt as to the knowledge of ultimate reality must include doubt as to our power of knowing God, epistemological agnosticism naturally has a bearing on the religious issue.

There are two types of agnosticism, which may be called dogmatic and provisional. The former is nearer to ancient scepticism, the latter represents an attitude which every one adopts towards certain things which they think are possible, but not demonstrated as true. This latter type is more in evidence at the present time.

Of the historical expressions of the more modern type of scepticism it will be sufficient to mention two, the theological and the secular. Sir William Hamilton, though a theist, declared that a God understood was no God at all, and that to think that God is as we could think Him to be is blasphemy. Hamilton held that human knowledge was limited to the relation between phenomena, and God was the Absolute on which the relative was founded. God was therefore outside all such relations and consequently unknowable. Mansel, a Dean in the Church of England, invoked Hamilton's metaphysical aid to prove that it follows we know God only by revelation. Herbert Spencer was influenced by Mansel's scepticism, whilst declining its remedy. God, he remarked, was 'a normal affection of the intellect', but one that had no logical justification. This marked the collapse of theological agnosticism.

The secular variety fared little better, whether in the form of positivism or secularism. Comte started from his own notion that there were three stages in the evolution of thought, theological, metaphysical and positive, and attempted to limit knowledge to the last, though he conceded to religion the compliment of constructing a positivist faith, i.e. the worship of humanity. The school was represented in this country, though with the death of Frederic Harrison the last well-known British positivist disappeared. The positivists knew, or thought they knew, the truth about the material world, and limited their scepticism to that concerning the spiritual world. The modern developments of physics have rendered the positivist position merely an historical curiosity, while the positivist religion collapsed through its own defects. A British movement influenced by positivism and by the atheism of Bradlaugh, while maintaining its independence of both, was the secularism of G. J. Holyoake, who suggested that mankind should limit itself to the secular as the only definite and important side of life. 'Strive', he said, 'for the secular improvement of the race and leave religion on one side, neither fighting for or against it, but allowing it to be the private concern of those who care to entertain it.' This, he claimed, would unite theist and atheist in that service of man which, if there were a God, is the best service of God. Of course, this attempt to limit knowledge is philosophically unjustifiable. But in any case, it is vain. There are many practical secularists who ignore God because they have no interest in Him. Holyoake made the mistake of trying to give reasons why God's existence might be admitted and ignored. But, as one of his critics remarked, this was as foolish a proceeding as to say there was a tiger outside, but its presence or absence made no difference to our going out-of-doors. In a word, secularism is as possible in practice as it is impossible in theory.

The Purpose of Philosophy

Criticism of Agnosticism

Modern scientific thought is swinging away from agnosticism. Arguments like those of Hamilton amount simply to the fact that reason cannot comprehend all that reality contains. But instead of that driving us to agnosticism we realize to-day that life is more than reason and that intellectual antinomy is no proof of unreality. Both psychology and physics, from different standpoints, have shown us the limits of reason, and hence the agnostic notion that we must believe only what is capable of rational explanation, has collapsed.

The older type of agnosticism is met also by a dilemma which is fatal to its assumption that the knowable and demonstrable are one. The dilemma is as follows. All knowledge depends on a basis of faith, for the premises of demonstration cannot be demonstrated. Either these are not knowable, in which case the knowable depends on the unknowable, or else they are knowable, in which case we must admit there can be knowledge that cannot be demonstrated.

Dogmatic agnosticism is an impossible attitude because it limits intellectual advance by an arbitrary ban placed on the possibilities of knowledge. We do not know what we can know until we try, and dogmatic agnosticism will not allow us to try. It would stop not merely religious investigation but scientific research into such subjects as telepathy, spiritism, intuition and the unconscious. But the assumption that real knowledge is limited to what can be rationally conceived has suffered badly through the new physics setting aside the classical conceptions and indicating that the ultimate characteristics of matter are, from the sense-standpoint, irrational.

Provisional agnosticism was brilliantly met by James's famous essay, *The Will to Believe*, which pointed out there was a twofold duty—to find out truth and avoid error. But to obtain the former involves risking the latter. The agnostic is a man so afraid of making a mistake that he risks missing the truth. James showed, both on moral and on practical grounds, that it was better to seek truth even at the risk of falling into error.

Agnosticism had a brief impetus in the days of the science v. religion disputes following Darwin. With the closing of that controversy and the new temper of scientists to religion, agnosticism has waned. It is no longer able to claim the support of science for its attitude. The modern temper is much more closely expressed in the words of Einstein. 'The scientist must see all the fine and wise connexions of the universe and appreciate they are not of man's invention. He must feel toward that which science has not yet realized like a child trying to understand the works and wisdom of a grown-up. As a consequence, every really deep scientist must necessarily have religious feeling.'

Chapter III
The Idea of God

GOD AND HUMAN REASON

The Beginnings of Theism

IT has been made clear that belief in God did not arise from any act of reasoning, nor yet from the necessity of questions concerning the origin of the world, but from grounds more closely connected with practical and emotional life. Long before man indulged in rational speculation concerning himself and the universe, the gods were an accepted fact in his beliefs, and to all intents and purposes, we may consider that the beginnings of rational theology are to be found in the religious teachers of ancient Greece. It is true that they were antedated by Indian thought, and by the system of Gotama Buddha, but it is hardly possible to decide how far either of these as it now is, was the expression of that age, or how far it has been modified by later tradition. It is equally true that the Hebrew prophets were the first genuine monotheists, but their belief in God was the outcome of religious experience rather than of any process of reasoning. It was a certainty that needed no apologetic or support from philosophy.

Plato certainly deserves to be called the first philosophical theist. To him the notion that there were no gods, or at any rate that such as there were, cared nothing for this world, were irrational beliefs. Yet so did he dislike the idea that divine justice could be swayed by a little superficial piety and a few offerings, that he desired to prohibit all private shrines and sacrifices. Plato's interest in the ordinary religious ideas of his day forbids us calling him a monotheist in a strict sense, yet, if as some of his most sympathetic expositors hold, he meant the Idea of the Good to be identified with God, he did reach an ultimate monotheism based on strictly rational grounds. To Plato it was the pure in thought rather than the pure in heart who should see God.

Aristotle's conception of God was much more abstract. To

The Philosophical Approach to Religion

him God was a philosophical principle pure and simple, pure intelligence, pure activity. As he regarded God and matter as alike self existent and eternal he cannot be called an absolute monotheist. Moreover, Aristotle's God is too supremely transscendent to be a personal or moral being. His arguments in favour of the conception of God he held, are at first glance not unlike those later designated the cosmological and teleological arguments. The one is based on the supposition that motion involves an immobile Prime Mover, 'movens sed immotum'. The other is based on the gradual perfecting of ends in Nature. Yet God is not the cause of the world, but rather the ideal towards which the world is shaping. Like Plato, Aristotle could not believe in an ideal which was not also a real. Hence God must exist, but there is no reciprocity between God and the world. He is neither its creator nor sustainer. Any illustration must be misleading, for there is no parallel that can be offered to this strangely one-sided relation between God and the world, but if we imagine a youth, taking some man who knows nothing of him as his model and ideal, and shaping his career upon that of his hero, we shall have some analogy of the state of things that exists between God and the world, according to Aristotle.

It is one of the ironies of history that the Middle Ages should have followed Aristotle's theism in preference to that of Plato, till the Reformation shook both the power of the Pope and of Aristotle, that strangely associated pair. But Plato was supposed to have denied the resurrection of the body, and to be guilty of complicity with pagan notions, and so the much more religious thought of a much more religious man was passed over, and the *Republic* virtually lost for a thousand years, in favour of the arid intellectualism of Aristotle's theology. Even so, the reconciliation between Aristotle's views and those of the Church needed all the finesse of the mediaeval theologian, and was but a patched up affair when all was said and done.

Stoic philosophy swung over to the deification of the universe, not, however, as a chance collocation of atoms, but as Providence, or God. Stoicism was thus in theory pantheism, though like other pantheisms, by no means always consistent. The Stoic optimism sprang from the same thought that the All was good, and hence whatever happened must also be good, and it was this which was responsible for the temper which now is popularly

The Idea of God

associated with the Stoic name. The Stoic was not a believer in the virtue of stubborn resignation. His supposed impassivity was due to the belief that all was good, and therefore preferences for one or other state of things were simply subjective choice amongst various kinds of good, so that it was beneath the dignity of manhood to press such preferences too far as if they were ultimately important.

We should not expect that Epicurean philosophy would add much to the doctrine of God, but in one respect at least, we are its debtors. It was the Epicureans who added to the divine attribute of reason, that of happiness. The New Testament reference to the Gospel of the Blessed God re-echoes a Homeric term, which might well be rendered 'The Happy God'. That the attribute happiness has been so little employed in Christian theology to denote the state of the Divine Mind, reflects upon the materiality of our conception of what constitutes happiness.

With the Neoplatonists' regression to Plato, there entered also an oriental and mystical element quite un-Platonic. God became the 'One Beyond Intelligence', attained only by mystical absorption. The beginning of mysticism is usually the end of philosophy, and after Plotinus nothing of note was added to the rational conception of God. In A.D. 529 Justinian suppressed the schools, and for a thousand years, philosophy was bound with chains. The development of the idea of God, no longer free, ran its course from the starting point of the traditional Hebrew notion, with St. Paul's modifications, and was kept, under due penalty, within the beaten track of theology.

The Growth of Christian Theism

It is not strange therefore that the idea of God remained stagnant. The storm centre was in the person of Christ rather than in the nature of the Deity. Yet even so, there was a certain movement towards a higher conception. Tertullian had thought of God as substantial, though not corporeal, but the doctrine of the pure spirituality of God gradually set aside any such idea, and whilst popular conceptions remained anthropomorphic, Augustine gave to theology his own idea of God, which was destined to become the dominant notion for many centuries. On the one side, it was metaphysical, for the Neoplatonists, as well as the Manichees, were represented in Augustine's philosophical pedigree. From the latter he obtained the notion of divine transcendence: from the former, the notion of divine immanence, rejecting in one case the dualism, and in the other the anti-rational mysticism, of his mentors. The other side of Augustine's conception of God was empirical, as the *Confessions* witness. To him, God was the immediately experienced reality that Christ was to St. Paul. From these two sources, never completely harmonized by Augustine, developed within the Church the metaphysical conceptions of God amongst the schoolmen, and the mystical conceptions of the saints.

Harnack may be right in stating that the two are sides of one Phenomenon according as the subjective or objective interest prevailed, but it remains that they developed largely independently. Nor did the Reformation make any essential contribution to the doctrine of God. No reaction contributes much to a point not acutely in dispute. Indirectly, through the breaking up of the monasteries, and the increased knowledge thereby made possible to the layman, the Reformation prepared for the independent thought that began to show itself in Hobbes and his successors. Yet Hobbes made no motion towards the atheism with which he was charged, and when he died, was buried with Christian rites as a Christian man, who, according to his friend Aubrey, 'would have the worship of God performed with musique'.

Subsequently there developed the habit of philosophers to make use of the idea of Deity to fill in the gaps in their systems, a practice which dates at least from Descartes. Spinoza united the Cartesian dualism of extension and thought into 'substance', a term which for him meant the ground of existence, and not of course the materialistic notion that the word possesses for us. Substance was God, and hence Spinoza was charged inevitably with pantheism, since he left nothing in reality save God. But Spinoza's pantheism was purely intellectual, and no man came nearer to resolving his mind into a thinking machine than he. Yet, as every Jewish child learns, as his first lesson in theology, that God is one, and that to love God with all his mind is the first duty of man, Spinoza was susceptible to the earliest influences of life when he taught that reality was one, and that 'the intellectual love of God' (amor intellectualis Dei), was the chief end of man.

The Idea of God

Leibniz, at the opposite extreme, both as a man and as a thinker, needed the idea of God, to save him from the effects of his own pluralism. For him, reality was composed of an infinite number of 'monads'. Each monad was a separate centre of experience, having no means of communication with other monads. This sandheap multiverse became a universe through the action of God, the central monad, who was the creator of the other monads. By means of 'pre-established harmony' God orders the intercourse and development of the monads, making the lower orders of creation His instruments, and the higher His agents. The universe is therefore a perpetual miracle, with God to perpetuate it.

Such philosophical conceptions, however, added nothing to the idea of God in the religious sense. They served only to make deeper the gulf between the God of metaphysics and the God of religion, that manifested itself in Augustine. Indeed, save for the identity of name, there is often nothing in common between the two. Yet Hegel, who identified the Absolute with God, seemed quite insensible to the incongruity of the proceeding.

THE FIRST QUESTIONINGS

IT was left to Hume to contest the whole question of the rational conception of God, but in doing so, he raised such controversy over the whole question of scepticism that the true implications of his doubt were obscured in his own age. Hume was neither the dangerous infidel of his enemies' imagination, nor the great philosopher his friends pictured. He never espoused atheism, nor did he deny that the universe implied God, though he asserted, with truth, that ordinary belief was not based on reason. The *Dialogues Concerning Natural Religion* give the essence of his position. In them a rationalist, that is to say, philosophical theist, a sceptic, and an orthodox believer, dispute the question of theistic belief. The argument is fairly sustained, and though to the reader it seems that the sceptic has the best of it, the concluding sentences express a preference for the views of the philosophical theist, a preference which Hume assured his friends was his own. There is no doubt at all that all rational grounds for belief in God were viewed by him with the utmost suspicion. Yet that suspicion was based on the inadequacy of

The Philosophical Approach to Religion

human reason to reach any such conclusions, not on the impossibility, or even the improbability, of God's existence. Hume, as Kant tells us, woke him from his 'dogmatic slumber', and it was the doubts of Kant, rather than of Hume, which threw the whole question of rational proof of God's existence into uncertainty. Yet Kant's doubts were based upon exactly the same grounds, namely the incapacity of reason. The difference lay in the fact that Kant's philosophy provided a systematic indictment of the powers of speculative reason in reaching transcendental conclusions, which Hume never gave. Moreover, Kant was by far the greater thinker, and whilst as dissatisfied with mere reasoning as was Hume, went beyond Hume in trying to replace the basis of reason with a basis of moral certainty. In short, Kant led the way towards the distinction between judgements based on matters of fact, and judgements expressive of values, and so was the first to introduce the argument from experience.

THE THEISTIC PROOFS

THE word 'proof' is far from being unambiguous. What is accepted as proof in a mathematical problem, a philosophical discussion, and in a court of law, is in each case quite a different matter. That explains why some have declared that the existence of God is a truth so evident that no proof of it is needed; whilst others have spent a lifetime in collecting and expounding such proofs; and others again have summarily declared that no proof is or can be possible. The theistic proofs belong to an age when scientific method in the modern sense was unknown, and when it would have seemed the height of impiety to speak of the existence of God as a hypothesis, despite Butler's insistence that probability was the guide of life.

We now recognize that the laws of nature are actually hypotheses which receive such confirmation in experience that they are accepted as true. The general notion of evolution is accepted by all modern thinkers, and yet it must remain a hypothesis. In seeking to demonstrate it, we meet with serious objections to which we can but reply that we are not in a position to supply facts that will satisfy them, but none the less, the positive evidence is sufficient to allow of the acceptance of the idea of evolution despite the gaps in its proof. It is not otherwise with

The Idea of God

the idea of God. In the strict sense it is incapable of proof, but equally of disproof. Yet we cannot prove the existence of ourselves, of other people, or of the external world. Nothing that is ultimate can be proved or disproved. In the technical sense of the term, the existence of God is a hypothesis. It is not possible to meet all the objections that can be raised against it, any more than one can meet those that can be raised against fundamental hypotheses of modern science. But a hypothesis is accepted not because it is necessarily undeniably demonstrated, but because it has the capability of explaining known facts, and sufficient evidence to give it preference over alternative explanations. It is in this way that we must regard the question of the Divine existence, and with this in mind we can proceed to the consideration of the traditional system of proofs.

All this was not apparent to the age in which the theistic proofs grew up. It seemed that reason must be capable of demonstrating God, and hence the four proof system was asked to carry a weight it could not bear. It failed, of course, to do so, and as a result there came a time when it fell into disrespect, although, despite Kant's criticisms, it remained in the forefront of textbooks of theology, and still occupies that place in some. It has been evident that of recent years, theology has grown apologetic of the 'proofs', and the tendency now seems to be unduly disparaging to their worth. If only they are taken for what they are, and not for what they are not, they remain not simply of historic, but of present importance. Manifest as are their defects, regarded as demonstrations, none the less they serve to express convictions which common sense will never cease to hold, and the very fact that though they have been slain times without number, they invariably succeed in rising again, indicates that whatever damage they may have suffered has not made them manifestly useless. What use remains in them may be best seen by asking ourselves exactly what is meant by proof in this case, and how far the four traditional arguments have validity as indicating reasons for belief in God's existence.

THE ONTOLOGICAL ARGUMENT

ANSELM (1033–1109) defined God as That than which a greater cannot be conceived (Aliquid quo nihil majus cogitari potest).

The Philosophical Approach to Religion

But to exist in actuality (in re) is greater than to exist in thought (in intellectu). He concluded, therefore, there must exist That than which a greater was inconceivable, both in thought and in actuality (Existit ergo procul dubio aliquid quo majus cogitari non valet, et in intellectu et in re). God therefore must be conceived as actually existent by the very definition of what God is.

Anselm did not remain long unanswered. A monk, Gaunilo, declared that he conceived an island, which, as more perfect than any existing island, must therefore be an actuality. Anselm met the argument by denying that it was legitimate to proceed from any existence in thought to existence in fact, but only in the one case of necessary existence in thought. That was the unique idea of the Greatest of all. If, said Anselm, the island were the greatest most perfect thing conceivable, the argument would apply to it, but it cannot be such. Kant's criticism does not advance in any way beyond that of Gaunilo. It merely substituted 100 dollars for the island and in exactly the same way suggested that the dollars must, as the best possible, be in Kant's bank for him. We must welcome the criticism as Kant's sole attempt at humour, rather than for its merits. Anselm's was far too acute an intellect to be so manifestly ridiculed. The fact that the argument appealed to Hegel as satisfactory more than sets aside the jest of Kant. Perhaps the fact that Lotze, who rejected Anselm's argument, admitted the truth of its conclusion, indicates the gist of the matter. The ontological argument does not express a logical, but a moral, certainty.

The reason for the failure of Anselm's argument as a logically necessary demonstration is that it proceeds from a necessity of thought to a necessity of fact. To say that if one thinks of God, one must think of an existent God, is true, but it does not follow that what is necessary to the consistency of one's thought must be regarded as existing in any sphere outside thought. It is necessary to think of a triangle under the Euclidean geometry as having certain properties, but such a triangle cannot exist, if we are to accept the modern idea of a curvature in space. Anselm's argument remains entirely in the sphere of thought, and though we cannot consistently shape the thought of God without including therein the idea of existence, we cannot therefore infer that such existence is independent of my thought.

Whilst this may be admitted, it does not close the issue, but

The Idea of God

rather raises another, namely what is the relation of my thought to reality? The idealist cannot concede the implication that seems to underlie what has been said above that there is a realm of objective reality, which our thought may comprehend as from the outside, but which is alien to thought. John Caird put the meaning of the ontological argument in this respect as follows: 'As spiritual beings, our whole conscious life is based on a universal self-consciousness, an Absolute Spiritual Life, which is not a mere subjective notion or conception, but which carries with itself the proof of its necessary existence or reality' (*Introduction to the Philosophy of Religion*, p. 159). Existence is relative to thought. The most convinced realist cannot *think* of something existing unthought of, yet, none the less, he professes to apprehend that such existence must be. Idealists reject that notion, and hence for them the sole reality is thought, and since our individual thought cannot of itself explain experience they must assume some universal thought as the prius of our thinking, and what is more, as the presupposition of anything whatever existing, if existence is relative to thought.

The ontological argument, therefore, is an indication of the necessity of the conception of the Absolute, rather than of God, for the whole question of the relation of such an Absolute to God is an open one. Hegel identified the two, but a thinker like McTaggart, who was under close influence from Hegel, denied that the Absolute was God, and concluded there was no God. Bradley regarded God as an appearance of, but less than, the Absolute. To some personal idealists, the Absolute is a society, God and souls. It is clear therefore that we cannot assume that even on this interpretation the argument yields a theistic conclusion.

Perhaps its best service is in what it suggests rather than what it says. It expresses, albeit in a defective way, the conviction that the ideal must be the real, that the greatest perfection we can conceive cannot be a phantom of our imagination, and in this, both Plato and Aristotle would join with us. Anselm began with the isolated idea of God and argued it must also be a reality. That is too summary, but the deeper issue remains, and that is whether we could conceive such an idea if the ground of our being, through which we receive the power to think, were simply some blind unthinking Life Force? To argue in this way

The Philosophical Approach to Religion

is to prove nothing, but it remains that some of our firmest convictions are those we cannot prove, and that intuitions may be more instructive than our intellectual notions. At any rate, the ontological argument represents something more than a figment of the subtlety of Anselm's day in which it was current amongst the theologians. It represents a thought that in some way or another has haunted the greatest of minds. Descartes, in the third Meditation, expresses his belief that the very notion of perfection cannot be the creation of our imperfect natures. In his day it was, of course, held that man was created as he now is, and hence it was easy to argue that the idea of God must have been implanted in his mind by the Creator at his creation. The conception of evolution has altered our ideas in this respect, but it still remains that the process of evolution has brought about the existence of our moral, spiritual, and aesthetic nature, and if the source from whence our being is derived possesses none of these things, we have surpassed our origins, and must ourselves be creators of what our own ground of existence lacks. This argument has been caricatured by saying that on the same lines we must assume God is evil, because man is. This, however, is not a parallel. We do not argue that if the Absolute is the ground of the finite the Absolute must be finite, and if we are ignorant, God must be ignorant to make us so. The created can be less than the Creator, but not more. In his evil, man is less than God, but if man were good and the ground of his being were not good, man would be more than God. That there can be something in the end of a process that in some way was not in the beginning, was a thought Aristotle found incredible, and though there are modern thinkers who believe that by some process of cosmic conjuring, an unspiritual reality can produce spiritual natures, or at any rate can produce beings who possess what it has not, this seems one of those miracles which must be as embarrassing to agnosticism as the miracles of belief are said by the agnostic to be to the believer.

The ontological argument fails if it is put as axiomatic proof, but if it be regarded as supporting the conviction of religious experience that the God it meets in the heart must be real and the greatest of realities, it still remains and always will remain, stripped of its scholastic garments, as the expression, however faulty technically, of a conviction that is unshakeable.

The Idea of God

THE COSMOLOGICAL ARGUMENT

THE cosmological argument is the expression of one of the fundamental common-sense convictions of mankind. Young children, as soon as they learn to make things themselves, begin to question about the making of the world, and apparently, even deaf mutes, like those in the cases reported by William James, entertain such a notion. The creative 'high gods' of many primitive peoples point to the same line of thought amongst them, for whatever may have been the origin of the idea, now, at least, the high god serves as an explanation of the making of things. It is this conviction that the universe is the work of a Power not ourselves, that underlies the cosmological argument. Put in logical form the argument runs as follows:

> Every event has a cause:
> *The universe is an event.*
> Therefore the universe has a cause.

The major premise is the 'principle of sufficient reason', usually set down as axiomatic, and at any rate not a statement that can be contested. The minor premise has been challenged by arguing that an infinite regress may be the explanation, but this is not to explain, but merely to burke explanation. The other method of objecting to the argument was that of postulating the eternity of matter. Modern science, however, has itself disposed of the idea that the atom can be eternal. It is radiating away into space. Every modern authority agrees that the universe in its present form cannot possibly have existed from eternity. Indeed many are prophesying its total extinction in the process of cosmic time, a prophecy which seems to disturb some Christian thinkers, despite its accord with the New Testament conception. Those who are disturbed by the argument that the universe will perish cannot wholly have freed their minds from that materialism of the senses that thinks the ultimate character of reality is material, not mental.

Objectors to the cosmological argument would be on safer ground if they insisted that the logical form set out above involved the fallacy of four terms in that the word 'cause' is used in it in two senses. In the premise it refers to the type of cause which is itself the effect of a preceding cause. In the conclusion, it refers to what is called a 'First Cause', which is not itself caused. Is it legitimate, therefore, to argue from the one type of cause to the other? If the universe is said to be unintelligible without a cause, is not the First Cause, itself uncaused, just as unintelligible a conception?

None the less, the argument has not been without its appeal because of its coincidence with a habit of our thought. Locke said its evidence was equal to mathematical certainty: 'there is no truth more evident than that something must be from eternity.' Kant was constrained to admit that it had 'a certain persuasive force not less with the speculative than with the common intellect'. The chief limitation of the argument however, lies in the very word Locke employs—'something'. As Lotze said, it yields a metaphysical conception of the unconditioned. What it indicates is an 'Absolute', not a God of any value to theism, and to identify the Absolute with God has already been said, when speaking of the similar identification in the ontological argument, to be seriously questionable. To identify even the First Cause, or ground of existence, as this argument does, with God the Father, is pure assumption. At best the argument asserts really no more than that the ordinary nexus of cause and effect is inadequate to explain reality as a whole. That may be granted, but to do so will not help theism very much. The idea that the argument explains the universe is negatived by the fact that it neither suggests why or when the universe arose. It merely throws us back upon a ground of reality, that must be assumed, but escapes all description. That such a ground is God may be true, but the argument does not prove it in the least.

The best use of the argument is in connexion with idealism. Dr. Rashdall urged that since science finds every indication that we must regard the universe as far older than man, and since idealism demonstrates the rationality of the assertion that matter cannot exist apart from mind, the conclusion must be drawn that there is a mind other than the mind of man for which the universe exists. To the idealist this is acceptable, but such a mind need not be that of God in the religious sense. It might be the mind of an Absolute, or the minds of a plurality of beings, and Rashdall, who admitted this, was driven to the further argument that pluralism failed to afford a satisfactory explanation.

The Idea of God

A further contention of the same thinker was that causality as found was merely succession, but as interpreted, it was activity. The only cause we actually experience is that of our own wills, and hence he argued that what was not caused by our wills, was reasonably to be attributed to the Divine Will, a contention that is in like case to the former argument. Idealism, therefore, still finds a place for both the ontological and, the cosmological arguments, and to those who accept the contention of idealism as to the dependence of matter upon mind, the arguments have a significance that escapes the realist. Yet even so, they lead towards, but do not reach, a theistic conclusion.

THE TELEOLOGICAL ARGUMENT

THE teleological argument has been presented in two ways, not always distinguished. It has been either from or to design. Some of the most eloquent passages in the Old Testament argue from design to the might and wisdom of God. The thinkers of ancient Greece were equally impressed by the evidence of design in nature. Anaxagoras argued therefrom for a divine intelligence, and Pythagoras anticipated certain modern thinkers in the opinion that God must be a mathematician. Plato used the argument in the *Timaeus*. Aristotle's own scientific studies in biology and physics convinced him of teleology. The growth of scientific knowledge within the last two centuries has not altered the impression in many minds. A naturalist like Agassiz could declare that thorough classification was an interpretation of the mind of God, and even so ardent a Darwinian and one so critical of theism as Sir Arthur Keith, can say, 'Design is manifest everywhere. Whether we are laymen or scientists, we must postulate a Lord of the Universe' (*Forum* Ap. 1930).

It was, however, in the eighteenth century that the argument was at its height of popularity. Divines and also scientists cited all manner of contrivances and adaptations in Nature as proof that a creator had designed them for that purpose, and though Hume reminded them of the ugly fact of dysteleology, that is to say, apparently malevolent or purposeless adaptations, he himself was sufficiently impressed to put into the mouth of Philo in the *Dialogues*, the opinion that 'a purpose, an intention, a design strikes everywhere the most careless, the most stupid thinker'.

The Philosophical Approach to Religion

Kant called the argument 'the clearest, oldest and best suited to human reason'. Little wonder that in the time of Paley and the Bridgwater treatises, the argument was considered impregnable. But with the coming of Darwin the type of adaptation upon which Paley relied came to be regarded in a wholly different light.

The earlier notion that Darwinism had exploded the grounds for believing in design, can no longer be maintained. For one thing, the time during which 'chance variations' might develop at random until by mere law of probability they could account for all existence, is far too short. The celebrated remark that six monkeys strumming unintelligently on typewriters could, granted cosmic millions of years, produce all the books in the British Museum, would on the laws of probability require so many millions that the whole age of the universe would be utterly insufficient for them to produce the merest fraction of a single book with absolute correctness. Much less can the time during which life has been upon the earth be enough to account for all the adaptations of Nature by mere 'chance' variation. Indeed, any who can believe this, must be capable of believing in something beside which the whole of the Arabian Nights would appear as a simple and credible narrative.

Darwin, needless to say, was much more cautious. He postulated certain variations as indefinite or accidental, because in our complete ignorance of the causes of variation, this course was as necessary as it is for an Insurance Company to deal with 'expected deaths' on the basis of probability. The assumption that this proceeding indicates that variations must be accidental manifestly begs the question. It is one thing, and perfectly legitimate, to ignore design for a special purpose, but quite another, and wholly illegitimate, to assume that thereby in some manner the question of the possibility of design has been settled.

Darwinism, then, offers no account of the arrival of the fittest, nor of that co-ordination of variations, without which any single variation would be of little use. It says nothing of the origin of adaptation; presuming indeed an initial adaptation of organism to environment to allow it a start in life, a basis on which further adaptation can take place.

The means by which this initial adaptation is conserved

The Idea of God

through the various stages of its existence was thought by Darwin to be chiefly 'natural selection'. That natural selection is an agency in evolution is indisputable, but the opinion of the majority of modern biologists seems to be that Darwin overestimated its importance, and that it cannot carry all the functions assigned thereto. It does not, in any case, help to explain why some organisms vary, whilst others have remained stable for an indefinite period, nor does it account well for the degenerative types of variation. In short, whilst Darwinism is fatal to the type of argument upon which Paley relied, it does not preclude belief in teleology. Indeed, in one respect at least it eases the situation, because instead of trying to prove, with the older type of argument, the perfection of nature, it is now possible to argue that there is a process towards perfecting, a design in the progress and direction of evolution. Certainly not every device of nature is manifestly perfect even for its own function. Helmholtz once said that the eye was so poor a piece of workmanship as an organ for sight, that any craftsman who made such an article would be worthy of dismissal. The conception of evolution at any rate relieves the apologist from meeting such an argument.

Moreover, consciousness certainly ministers to the process of natural selection. Man survived solely because of his superior mental powers, though pitted against foes, both in physical and in animal nature, much stronger than he was. If consciousness serve in the process, there is no ground for denying that it could also serve in the planning of that process.

During Darwin's lifetime, Asa Gray wrote an article in *Nature*, in which he said that Darwin's great service to natural science was in bringing back to it teleology, so that instead of teleology being opposed to morphology, the two were joined. In a letter to Gray, Darwin wrote, 'What you say about teleology pleases me especially, and I do not think that any one else has ever noticed the point' (*Life of Charles Darwin*, pp. 291, 297).

Darwin apparently overlooked the fact that Huxley had said the same thing some five years previously, adding that whilst Darwin had destroyed the older type of teleology, there was a wider teleology, not touched by the hypothesis of evolution, but based on its fundamental proposition. As to the existence of design pointing to a designer, Darwin seems never to have been

The Philosophical Approach to Religion

able to make up his mind. He said that the notion of the universe and ourselves arising from chance seemed so impossible of conception that it was to him the chief argument for the existence of God, yet he at once added that he was not able to decide the value of any such argument. He denied that he had ever been atheistic in thought, though at times, but not always, he had been agnostic. Evolution he declared to be not incompatible with theism, but added once more that there were differing ideas of what was meant by God. The existence of suffering pressed heavily on his mind, and seemed to be a strong argument against an intelligent 'first cause', yet he owned that when he wrote the *Origin of Species* that conviction of an intelligent source of Nature was strongly with him. 'I deserve to be called a theist' he remarked. Yet he admitted that the impression waned, and realizing the hopelessness of coming to any final conclusion, feared he must be 'content to remain an agnostic'. He admired the beautiful hinge of a bivalve, but could not argue that, like the hinge of a door, it must have been made by an intelligent being. His position is expressed in a conversation with the Duke of Argyll, when he admitted that the wonderful contrivances of Nature at times seemed to him with overwhelming force to point to mind behind them, and yet at other times the impression seemed to vanish. In short, whilst Darwin was not anti-teleological, he was unable to convince himself either that such design did or did not imply a designer.

Darwin's position is indicative of the situation generally as regards the teleological argument. Those who object to teleology on the ground of a mechanistic theory of life in chemico-physical terms have not strengthened their position within recent years. Indeed, some seem inclined to try to join this view with the notion that there can be an inner teleology in the self-regulation of the organism. The theory of Driesch that postulates an 'entelechy', not chemico-physical, as the formative, and a 'psychoid' as the directive element in life, has found small acceptance. Yet the thorough-going mechanist is in worse case. As Whitehead says (*Science and The Modern World*, p. 21), 'What is the sense of talking about a mechanical explanation when you do not know what you mean by mechanism?' Modern science admits it does not know, and the ambitious hope of a mechanistic explanation of life, therefore, is specula-

The Idea of God

tion, not science, and moreover a speculation that, in the recent developments, seems further than ever from establishing itself.

The position, therefore, seems to be that the evidence for teleology in Nature is impressive, but the question as to what can be concluded from such evidence is still very open. Prof. Norman Kemp Smith in a pamphlet called *Is Divine Existence Credible?* has argued recently that the design argument ignores the distinction between the natural and the artificial product, and that it is illegitimate to argue from the one to the other. Further, that to conceive of God as designer is to do so in terms of attributes proper only to a creaturely being. Design implies foresight, and foresight is manifest in repetitive activities, and does not apply to true creation. We do not possess even the beginnings of an understanding of what is implied by creativity in the ultimate sense. Hence he concluded that to argue from what is presented to us in Nature *to* design, is illegitimate. He equally objects to arguing *from* design, because the impression of design in Nature which our minds receive is due not to the actual facts presented to us, but rather to a certain traditional way of seeing them. Actual Nature, in the raw, does not present to us any overwhelming evidence of design, but a mixture of teleology and dysteleology, of adaptation and destruction in blind impartiality. If the data do not enable us to argue to design, how can they serve as a basis for arguing from design?

Professor Kemp Smith accepts the theistic position, but on the ground of immediate experience of God. His objections to the teleological argument are not influenced by objections to a theistic conclusion, and represent an impression most theists acknowledge, that, even if we accept the fact of design in Nature, and overlook the evidence for dysteleology as insufficient to outweigh the evidence for design, we are not led to any inevitable conclusion as to a creative mind, much less to a God of value to religion. Yet notwithstanding, when we have a belief in God, Nature does contribute to that belief, and few things more strengthen it than to see 'how manifold are thy works.' The book of Job is a classical expression of this sense, and yet it cannot be maintained that the author received his faith from contemplation of the works of Nature, and the appeal of the argument either from or to design lies just in that sense of God in Nature from which Darwin even could never divest himself,

The Philosophical Approach to Religion

and was to Wordsworth the most evident of truths. Moreover, it is probable that primitive religious ideas arose from contemplation of the numinous, the 'mana-possessing' phenomena of Nature. Whilst the teleological argument does not prove God's existence, it does put into words an impression that none of us wholly escape.

James Ward, in *Naturalism and Agnosticism*, in a treatment that may be called classic, lifted the question of teleology to a plane much above that of wrangling as to the purpose of certain biological adaptations. He contended that the idea of the unity of Nature, of law, regularity, and causality are alike formed from the facts of self activity. In ourselves we find the key that unlocks the universe to our understanding. If things conform to thought, Nature is in that sense teleological. She has permitted adaptation between herself and our minds that are able to comprehend her ways. Moreover, the very idea of mechanism in the name of which some would dismiss purpose, is the creation of our purpose to understand the working of Nature.

Mr. Bertrand Russell, in a candid moment, admitted it was a strange mystery that we could judge the works of our unthinking mother Nature. In our philosophy and science we are so accustomed to assuming that we can, that we do not always realize how ungrounded this assumption appears when we permit ourselves to dally with the idea of a blind purposeless force behind the phenomena of the universe. We ought, in such case, to make it clear that this blind force has kindly been sufficiently capable of making adaptations that it has adapted our intelligence to discover its nature. If not, someone may assume, as indeed he would be well justified in assuming, that possibly, this blind force had made us so that we are forever doomed to think we can attain the truth concerning it, when there is no such thing as truth at all, or that all our ideas about existence and its grounds should be forever foreordained to falsity. Of course if that were believed, there would be no further purpose in writing about the blind life force. So it is quietly understood that the rules of the game, in order to permit debate, allow of one miracle only, that of a blind purposeless force adapting its nature to the comprehension of human minds, but that we must be no more teleological than that. Yet it is manifest that this concedes the whole point at issue, and

The Idea of God

makes the conception of a blind purposeless force at once suspect. In order to argue against the existence of purpose and adaptation, it is needful to beg beforehand one great adaptation, that between our minds and reality. Yet the grounds upon which this is granted cannot be restricted to that alone. That there is adaptation between truth and reality, and yet between no other value and reality, is a manifest begging of the question. Once raise the teleological issue, and you cannot stop until it has involved the whole question of man, his mind, his ends and values and the universe which bore him. A purposeless universe leaves truth as bereft of ground as all moral and spiritual values.

Bergson's protest against a radical finalism is another matter. He considers that it is at root the same as mechanism. It is as if one looked at the same field from both ends of the telescope. Looked at from the beginning, it appears that Nature is mechanistic, proceeding from an initial energy inexorably propelling the system of evolution forward. Looked at from the end, it appears to a radical finalism as one far-off divine event to which the whole creation inevitably moved. To Bergson's strong belief in indeterminism, the one conception seems as fixed and unalterable as the other, though of the two, he prefers finalism. But there is no need for those who believe in purpose in existence to adopt any such radical finalism. Reality may still be in the making. In Bergson's latest work we find he has decided that the 'élan' either is or comes from God, so that, apparently, on his own showing, belief in God is not necessarily committed to belief in any utter and radical finalism.

It is enough to say that the teleological argument is an expression of that sense of purpose in life and in the universe of which we can never entirely, or even consistently, rid ourselves. It is not a proof of God and yet it once more adds, as do the other theistic arguments, to the cumulative evidence for our belief in God. If it be said that it is the belief that collects the evidence, rather than the evidence that reinforces the belief, it matters little. Was it not Bradley who said that metaphysics was the finding of reasons for what we believed by instinct? The greatest obstacle to teleology is such facts as parasitism, which, whilst they do not touch the question of design, do challenge the morality of it. Yet even so, much parasitism is relatively harmless, and that which is noxious is after all small compared with the beneficent design of Nature. It is best frankly to admit the objection, without admitting that it is fatal in itself to the general conception of teleology.

THE MORAL ARGUMENT

THE action of Kant in rejecting all the usual 'proofs' of theism is well known, but as regards his rejection of the ontological argument, it is not always realized that in an early treatise Kant set forth a variant of that argument which at the time impressed him, as the only possible proof of the existence of God. In his thesis for a degree, he first set forth a proof that there is a being whose existence is antecedent to the possibility of the existence of itself and of all else, and some eight years later, in the treatise referred to above, he gave practically the same argument, that possibility must presuppose actuality, and hence the real is the only basis upon which we can presume the possibility of anything. Kant maintained that position, at any rate, up to 1770, for the argument occurs in a slightly different form in his inaugural lecture as professor in that year. When we come to the *Critique of Pure Reason* (1781), Kant dismisses Anselm in a summary manner, and proceeds to demolish the other arguments. That of the cosmological 'proof' he sets aside by saying that if all that is known can be shown to have a cause, the principle of causality need go no further. He also objected to the notion of a first cause as really involving the same notion as that he had dismissed in the ontological argument, of a being necessarily existent. Kant has here turned with vengeance on the Kant of a dozen years before. He was more respectful to the teleological argument, but regarded it as a special case of the cosmological. He asserted further that we could but see partial design and could not assume its universality, and at most we could not prove more from design than the probability of an intelligent demiurge. Kant left the question, convinced he had destroyed the old speculative theology, but with plans of replacing it by a new theology which should be based on surer foundations.

After all this destructive dynamite used upon the old foundations, one might expect something of convincing strength in

The Idea of God

the argument that Kant puts in their place. Yet the moral argument on which he solely relies cannot be said to be strongly put. Kant's Scottish-Prussian ancestry and early training had left him with an inescapable sense of moral duty. To him such duty was the most obvious of facts. He knew too little of the evil of life to believe in the possibility of such a view being seriously challenged. He was convinced that duty could not be accounted for by the phenomenal world, and hence presupposed a free transcendental and ultimately real self, and for this and similar selves, immortality, in order that the moral ideal should be attainable. All this however implies that it is morally necessary to believe in God, for without God there is no guarantee that this inexorable sense of duty, the duty of seeking the 'summum bonum', is not an illusion. Kant could not conceive that any such possibility could be. Duty cannot be illusory. It speaks with an authority that nothing else possesses. The moral life would be an insoluble enigma if it were impossible to reach the summum bonum. That virtue should in the end coincide with happiness, that our duties should prove themselves to be divine commands, we must assume the existence of God, as a postulate of practical reason. Kant is sure that 'unprejudiced reason' must acknowledge this.

All this is more creditable to Kant's character than to his intelligence. There is a simplicity that is almost naive in imagining that this plea can replace all that Kant had jettisoned in the usual theistic arguments, or that it would convince those who were unconvinced by them. The sceptic has but to explain away moral obligation, or to attach it to social sanctions, and Kant cannot use his argument against him. Kant wanted to believe in God. He had dismissed the idea that reason could afford a ground for that belief. His own sense of duty led him to attach more importance to a deduction from it than such a deduction could carry. At best Kant shows that 'it is a mad world, my masters', if duty is a will o' the wisp. Yet that is precisely the characteristic of the universe of some of our modern pessimists. To Kant's impassioned 'It cannot be,' they reply 'Why not? As a matter of fact it is.' Curiously, too, the inwardness of Kant's argument is exactly that of the ontological argument he dismissed, the conviction that the ideal must be the real. Kant, instead of trying to prove this, as

Anselm did, by logic, asked us to consider it necessitated by moral sense. The abiding value of Kant's contribution to theism lay not in the argument he gave, but in the fact that he set forth clearly the principle of value for the first time, and drew attention to the inconsistency of believing in a rationally explicable universe which shows itself totally indifferent to moral and spiritual values. The vast majority of mankind, thinking and unthinking alike, cannot reconcile the felt authority and urgency of the moral sense, with the idea of an indifferent purposeless universe, or believe that a moral nature in ourselves can spring from an unmoral ground of our being. If that cannot be claimed as a rationally demonstrable truth, it can at least be called a moral certainty.

Other forms of the moral argument for theism have been more impressive than that of Kant. Butler's celebrated remark that if the power of conscience were comparable with its authority, it would govern the world, reappeared in the presentation of the moral argument by Martineau in his *Study of Religion*. 'Just as in perception we are immediately introduced to an *other than ourselves that gives us what we feel*, so in the act of conscience we are introduced to *a Higher than ourselves which gives us what we feel*' (Vol. ii. p. 27). In each case Martineau thought that our natural trust in our powers justified the conclusion, adding that he cared little whether such a conclusion was supposed to be intuitive or inferred. It would probably have added to the strength of the argument had he remained true to his own intuitionism here, for the inference can readily be disputed in several ways, for example by submitting that the higher than self is, as Durkheim and others think, society.

Dean Rashdall in the *Theory of Good and Evil*, and more briefly in *Philosophy and Religion*, has afforded a strong presentation of the moral argument by insisting that moral law is not subjective, but objective and absolute. Unless we are prepared to maintain that it is better to save life than to kill, only so long as men think so; that unselfish acts are better than selfish only so long as that view can command a majority of human opinions, we are committed to belief in an objective element in morality. But absolute morality does not exist in material things nor in individual minds. It presupposes a moral ideal eternally valid for mind, and such mind can be only the

The Idea of God

mind of God. If not a postulate of all morality, belief in God is at least a postulate of any sound morality. Rashdall, however, did not consider that this was enough in itself, and supplemented the argument by another based on the idealism which was his position philosophically, the argument for the divine existence to which reference was made above when speaking of the cosmological argument.

This is no doubt the best presentation of the moral argument, though it is more convincing by far to those who accept the idealistic position in philosophy. Yet even here we find idealists like McTaggart who solve the problem of reality's relation to mind, by adopting a pluralistic system. He contended (*Some Dogmas of Religion*, p. 251) that idealism is not necessarily committed to the position that nothing can exist except for a mind. It may also be maintained that nothing exists except minds and yet this does not imply that all that is true must be known to those minds. There are propositions true about ourselves of which we are not aware, and there may be propositions of which no one is aware, which are none the less true. McTaggart admits that to Rashdall's type of idealism the inference of an omniscient mind is justified, but declares that this is not the only type of idealism. It is very difficult, however, to see in what possible sense such propositions as McTaggart mentions can be said to exist, and he does not in any way enlighten us.

Other ways of meeting the moral argument have sought to attach morality to society. It is said for example that morality is relative, that we find 'the crimes of Clapham chaste at Martaban'. This, however, refers to the fact that there are moral standards which differ in different parts of the world. That right and wrong are two entirely different things is agreed alike both at Clapham and Martaban. It is suggested that morality is of social origin, being the laws of the tribe, or the result of the 'reality principle' enforced against the 'pleasure principle', as certain psycho-analysts put it. But as society did not make itself or its instincts and sentiments, this argument does not carry us far. If it be said that our ideas of God being of social origin therefore cannot refer to God, it is a palpable 'non sequitur', and the same applies to the notion that morality, since it arises in a social order, cannot refer beyond that order.

The Philosophical Approach to Religion

Some, however, hold that morality is purely of social significance, pertaining to the earthly well-being of the tribe or nation, tending to the equilibrium of society. That may be true as far as the immediate purpose of morality is concerned, but it does not touch the question as to the reasons why mankind is so constituted nor does it explain the difference in the insistence of moral laws as compared with social custom and etiquette.

Like the other theistic arguments, the moral argument proves most to those who already believe in God. To say so is not to admit that therefore its evidence is invalid. Symptoms in the condition of a patient indicate much more to the medical man than to the patient himself. It must always be that those who have inner knowledge will recognize significance in evidence that others do not see. But just as the medical man cannot rely on the evidence that convinces him to prove equally convincing to his patient, so the theistic arguments remain evidence for a theistic interpretation of life rather than 'proofs' that must be accepted by all capable of thought on the subject.

Belief in God as its own guarantee

We end therefore as we began. No proof that God exists has yet been given. None can be given in the ordinary sense of the word proof. Yet we cannot prove what we all profess to believe, that we ought to do right. For, as Bradley said, to ask why we should do right is an inadmissible question, since it presumes that there is that other than the right for the sake of which we should do it, that the right is a means to some other end than itself. But as Gwatkin put it (*Knowledge of God*, i. p. 10): 'The existence of God is not the less certain for being the necessary postulate of every argument instead of being the logical conclusion of one argument.' The philosophy of religion does not seek for proof of God's existence. Yet curiously, a particular argument that hung on as a kind of camp follower to the formal theistic arguments of the older text-books of theology, that known as E Consentu Gentium, is in some ways the most impressive consideration of all. To argue that the universality of belief in some kind of god or gods proves that such there be, is so obviously false as to require no refutation, yet if the unanimous testimony of the human race, wise and

The Idea of God

unwise, throughout all stages of culture, means nothing, and is a palpable delusion, it is hard to say what can save us from utter scepticism about any form of human knowledge. If we take experience as a basis for philosophy, we cannot ignore religious experience, and perhaps after all there is no better evidence for belief in God than the age-long quest of man for God. If that quest has been for a sheer illusion, it is more than the most colossal error, nay stupidity, of man, it is the most poignant tragedy of the human race. Belief in God does not rest upon logical considerations, and finds no guarantee in them. Such guarantee as it possesses lies in itself. That guarantee it has afforded to the overwhelming majority of mankind in all races and ages, and those who through their own experience of life have found God therein, look at that vast background of their fellows, knowing that nothing logic can offer can afford any surer confirmation.

GOD'S NATURE AND ATTRIBUTES

FROM the days of Animism till now, the nature of God has been thought of as spirit, more or less consistently, according to the mental development concerned. The Wahhabi sect of Islam is said to hold that God has a corporeal form, whilst the seven attributes of God, as orthodox Islam conceives them, add to knowledge, will, power and mercy, the attributes of sight, speech, and hearing. Even Tertullian held that God was substantial, though not corporeal. Nor is it possible to draw any very sharp distinction between His nature, attributes, and what are sometimes called 'predicates', such as creation and providence. Such distinctions have no special value, and we may content ourselves with a rapid characterization of the ideas usually expressed in the theistic representation of God.

To call God infinite may mean simply the negation of the finite, and in that sense does not carry us far. But the mathematical conception of infinity means much more than this mere negation of finite characteristics, and in similar manner the notion of infinity as applied to God may denote the complete, self-existent, self-determined ground of reality, an Absolute. But this will raise the vexed question of the relation of the Absolute to the God of religion, and theism should have

The Philosophical Approach to Religion

learnt by now to be wary of any facile identification of the two. The gain of such an identification, if it be possible, is likely to be outweighed by what must be jettisoned to secure it. The reaction from the notion of a finite God and pluralism nearly always lands in a monism that is either deistic or pantheistic, and equally sterile in all religious values, whichever it be. The whole question brings back the difficulty of doing justice to the facts of divine and human existence. The philosophies that give all that is claimed for God leave nothing over for man, whilst the humanistic and pluralistic philosophies seem to allow too little to God. For theism, the conception of an infinite God seems of value only when it is limited, despite the paradox of limiting an infinite. Yet we have learnt from Einstein to speak of an infinite-finite universe, and this may be some sort of precedent for speaking of the infinity of God as denoting that God is the ground of the finite, and limited by nothing other to His own nature, in short an infinite-finite God whose limitation is self-imposed. God lays down His own equations, but having done so, He must abide by them, for the very reason that the real cannot be conceived as self-contradictory, and the nature of God as the ultimate reality, creates its own inevitable way of expression. In this way, a place can be found for man as well as God in the universe, and to insist on infinity as meaning more than this, seems to be zeal for a meaningless word.

Similar difficulties attend the ascription of such attributes at omniscience and omnipresence, and omnipotence. Omniscience presents a 'prima facie' contradiction in that an omniscient Being cannot have the experience of a certain fact that is only too common in human experience, being in error and thinking all the while that the error is true. An omniscient God may know what it means to human beings to err, but there is a peculiar quality of actual error which He cannot have experienced. It presents an equal difficulty as regards human freedom, for knowledge of the future implies the predetermination of that future, and none of the suggested methods by which the difficulty has been met bears any marks but those of special pleading, not to say equivocation. A thorough-going doctrine of omniscience, linked with omnipresence, leads to pantheism, and nowhere else. These attributes may be taken as a strong expression of the divine immanence, but beyond

The Idea of God

that, they lead only to a position embarrassing to any genuine theism.

Of omnipotence, Ward said (*Realm of Ends*, p. 354): 'Omnipotence, I fear, is one of those question-begging epithets that everybody uses and nobody defines. Thus it is not uncommonly taken to imply not merely the power to do whatever it is possible to do, but also the power arbitrarily to determine what shall be possible, in short, that omnipotence absolutely excludes impossibility. . . . Metaphysics of this sort is not to be met by argument.' If we press the idea of omnipotence beyond that of the power freely to choose its own conditions, we must reach that type of metaphysics to which Ward referred. Absolute omnipotence is a contradictory conception. No one can argue that God can at the same time ordain that all men shall be saved, for example, and some not saved. Nor is there any meaning in stating that God can make an odd number divide evenly by two. Every one in practice excludes certain things from the range of omnipotence, and it seems unwise to adhere strictly to a word which cannot be given any general connotation. If we use the term it must be in the sense that omnipotence refers to the power of God harmoniously with His own nature, to decide what shall be, and even so, if we believe in the reality of free will, we must add that God decided to limit His powers by the gift of that power to man. Such attributes as eternity and immutability can be only relatively ascribed. Eternity can be taken to mean that God is above the limitation imposed on man by time, and immutability that the character of God is permanently self-consistent. An absolutely immutable God would imply that all beside Himself was 'appearance', not reality, and even so, there would be the insoluble problem why this immutable being permitted the appearance that obscures his immutability. An immutable being is the last source one would imagine as a creator of the finite. The difficulties of ascribing the attribute of wisdom have been seen in our discussion of the idea of design.

Such attributes as justice, mercy, holiness, belong to the religious rather than the philosophical conception of God, for they are based on religious experience rather than upon reasoning, and represent the conviction that the Ground of our being possesses in Himself our highest values.

The Philosophical Approach to Religion

The philosophy of religion, however, must regard the testimony of religious experience, just as philosophy generally regards the testimony of sense experience in its account of reality, and most philosophers have accepted experience, in its concrete sense, as the datum for philosophy. Are there any facts to which all religious experience testifies, facts which can be regarded as objective to religious experience? I think there are, and that in these we have the best attested characteristics of the divine. If we call them at once love, personality and goodness, we shall seem to be fantastically far from fact, yet in a certain limited but none the less definite sense, all three are at least implicit in germ in all religious experience.

The very fact that all religion presupposes that the object addressed will conceivably be favourable to the worshipper is the germ of the idea that God is love. Even the most degraded form of devil worship proceeds on the assumption that the spirit addressed can be placated and made for the once at least favourable to those who approach it. It is in this more than in anything else that it is possible to distinguish religion from magic. In the higher forms of religion we pass from the idea of a god intermittently kindly to a God by nature loving to man, but the lower forms exhibit the same idea in a lesser way. That God is love, in the sense, at least, that there is in reality a power or tendency sympathetic to human values, seems the essential postulate of all forms of religion. Though Buddhism is the anomaly amongst religions, it presumes that the goal set before the devotee can be gained. Not even Buddhism can envisage a permanent misfit between human existence and its ideals. But in Buddhist lands themselves, what we might call academic Buddhism, the type of creed that is described in textbooks, does not function as a religion for the mass of the people, who have either animistic or other additions and accretions to it, so that one is justified in leaving Buddhism aside in such a matter.

It is also true that all forms of working religion regard the God or gods as personal, at least in the one sense that justifies that epithet, namely as responsive to man in the way that human beings can be responsive. The sense of a response from the God to the worshipper implies in its degree communion between the two, and we can have communion in the real sense

The Idea of God

only between other minds and our own. The higher animals have some community of mind with ourselves and the companionship of man and his dog can reach what is truly a kind of communion, though the most enthusiastic observer of bees, ants and wasps can scarcely claim communion with the creatures he studies. The difference is one of mentalities. We speak of communion with Nature, but that is a form of communion with our own personalities, for we select the aspect of Nature with which we 'commune', and it is certainly not the red tooth and claw she exhibits. In other words, we commune not with Nature as a whole, but with that part of natural manifestations which appeals to our own mood.

If there is no communion with God, religious experience is a colossal hallucination. Against such a view is arrayed the unanimous testimony of religion in all times and places. That at least is enough to make us respect the attribution to God of 'personality', in the sense of response such as persons make. This no doubt is far from what personality can and should mean, but the attribute personal raises philosophic difficulties, such as Lotze appreciated when he said the doubt was whether we were personal, not whether God was. In other words, does the term personality in its human connotation hinder rather than help, if applied to God? Yet despite the difficulties, personality represents the highest form of spiritual expression known to us, and therefore has more appropriateness than any other as an attribute of God. Religious experience justifies one aspect of the term, and so long as it is not pressed too far, it remains the best of the words we can employ to characterize what we mean by God.

The ascription of moral goodness to God is an extension of that postulate of all religion just mentioned, that God is good in the sense of good to His worshippers, for if He were not, they would not try to win His favour. From this elementary idea of capricious favouritism to the idea of settled goodness is a long journey, but one upon which thought can hardly halt, once the journey has begun. In addition, all that was said of the supremacy of our moral sense reinforces the idea of a God morally good, and makes goodness an inevitable attribute of God.

To sum up then, we may say that the attributes we give to

The Philosophical Approach to Religion

God represent the necessarily imperfect ways of characterizing what our reason and our personal experience reveal to us of Him. Those, like infinity, omnipotence and the like, which are ascribed on rational grounds, are open to many objections on the same grounds, and though they have their use, they are not essential to the religious conception of God, save as denoting the sense of the power and otherness of God which comes in all religious experience. The attributes of love, goodness, and responsiveness, which are the chief justification for applying the term personal to God, are in stronger case, as they are supported not simply by reason, but by that commerce of the human soul with God which is the centre of religion. Theological attributes of God are always somewhat artificial conceptions, but those qualities which religious experience ascribes to God as the result of the relationship with Him which is given in religious experience, have at least empirical evidence to support them. To speak of God as good means much more than to speak of Him as infinite, and from the practical standpoint of human needs, is far more important. The extent of the divine power is a lesser matter, but the whole of the religious relation depends on the quality of the divine will. A finite God who loves man is vastly better than an infinite God who ignores him.

Some Modern Quasi-Theisms

In one of Galsworthy's stories the remark is made that every one nowadays believes in God, the only question being whether God is a person, or a conviction that right must come out uppermost. That is not far from being true. Atheism is as dead amongst the learned as amongst the ordinary people. Agnosticism is the refusal to think about the subject, or at best a reaction against the difficulties in the way of thinking it out, and an attempt to escape them by suspending further inquiry. Those who think, seldom fail in some way to believe in a God, but there are at least two or three types of modern philosophical thought that include a doctrine of God which cannot be called the Christian doctrine, nor in any ordinary sense the usual theistic belief, but which might perhaps be called quasi-theistic. It is not needful to include the ventures of certain psychoanalytic writers in this direction, for they have forgotten that, as a descriptive science, psychology must not trespass on meta-

The Idea of God

physical issues. They have assumed their conjecture that God is an expression of desire, or the father-image, carries with it the corollary that therefore He does not objectively exist. That, of course, is entirely unwarranted, and one must presume that only lack of acquaintance with philosophical matters, on the part of those whose training has been in psychology or biology, accounts for the error. It is not possible to examine their theses here. Let us, 'without prejudice', concede that they are right, and that it is the affective and emotional side of man's mind, rather than the rational, that has given to him his idea of God. It then follows that we must seek the connexion between this and man's apprehension of what is ultimately real, an issue to which as far as I know, not one of them has turned. Nor has any faced this question, that if we assume our rational beliefs to give us a true account of what is real, on what ground can we limit that apprehension to the rational, and exclude the emotional? If any such grounds do exist they are certainly not psychological, and of all men, the psychologist should be the last to assume that reason is the sole gateway to reality.

Apart from this type of theory, there are a couple of exceedingly interesting quasi-theisms at the present, in the conceptions put forward by Whitehead and by Alexander. Whitehead is by no means easy to interpret, and his expositors, recollecting how many have been the mistakes made by their fellows, must approach with caution. But at any rate, Whitehead has no place in his system for the ordinary idea of God the Maker of heaven and earth. His ultimate category is creativity, which is 'hylē' rather than mind, pure unformed activity, with God as the first created fact, proceeding from it in a manner reminiscent of the Arian doctrine of Christ as the firstborn of creation. This is the primordial nature of God. It is in consequence of this that there are any existent events as distinct from the primaeval abstract creativity. God is not the creator of the existent order, but rather its precondition, for not until boundless creativity was limited by the appearance of this first fact, God's primordial nature, could there be anything subsequent. God is not, says Whitehead, before, but with, all creation. In this respect God is like Aristotle's prime mover itself immobile. In short, at this stage God is simply a metaphysical necessity to Whitehead's system, an abstraction to

The Philosophical Approach to Religion

which Whitehead is certainly not justified in applying the personal pronouns in the way he does. It represents a way of mediating between the utterly uncharacterizable 'creativity' and the actual order of existence.

But Whitehead attributes to God, as well as this primordial nature, a consequent nature, which, unlike the primordial nature, is conscious, and represents the measure of the order attained in the process of world development. But once again we are not to think of the consequent nature of God as representing the creative source of the world order. It is 'his judgement on the world. He saves the world as it passes into the immediacy of his own life.' 'He does not create the world, He saves it, more accurately He is the poet of the world with tender patience leading it by his vision of truth, beauty and goodness' (*Process and Reality*, p. 490).

Lest we should read into such language a more familiar conception of the idea of God, it will be well to quote the antitheses which Whitehead gives us as his final summary. It is as true to say the one as the other of each of these statements. God permanent and the World fluent: the World permanent and God fluent. God one and the World many: the World one and God many. God in comparison with the World is actual eminently: the World in comparison with God is actual eminently. The World is immanent in God: God is immanent in the World. God transcends the World: the World transcends God. God creates the World: the World creates God. It is evident that Whitehead's doctrine has little in common with ordinary theism. The difficulty of apprehending his meaning is not a little due to the fact that he combines the mentality of a philosopher with the temperament of a poet, and it is not always easy to say when the poet gets the better of the philosopher, or the philosopher of the poet.

In comparison with Whitehead's *Process and Reality*, Alexander's *Space, Time, and Deity* presents a simple idea. In a word, it may be expressed by saying that in the beginning was space-time and in the end will be God. God is the ideal order towards which the universe is tending, coming to be, rather than existent; after, rather than before, all things. Alexander's idea of God is a reversal rather than a denial of the normal theistic conception.

The Idea of God

A third view until recently would have been placed beside these, had not Bergson in *Les Deux Sources de la Morale et de la Religion*, made his 'creative energy' capable of a theistic explanation. Previously no one could say whether it might not represent the barest abstraction. But those who have watched the trend of Bergson's thought will not be surprised by his latest declaration that this creative energy either is or proceeds from the Living God revealed in Christ and in the mystic experience, and prepared for by the Hebrew prophets. God is creative love. Bergson has not yet related his views to Christian theism, but it is evident that there cannot be any very great divergence on these lines. We are left therefore with Whitehead and Alexander as representative of ideas of God irreconcilable with ordinary theism.

There seems to be this in common between the two thinkers, that both revolt from the notion of a perfection behind all things which somehow has allowed the disintegration of itself in the evil and imperfection of the actual world. Alexander's views seem paradoxical in assuming that the process can transcend its source, and the imperfect set itself towards and attain the ideal. But it should be said that both theism and this type of thought have to face the same difficulty. For theism which starts from the idea of a perfect God, the problem is to explain the coming to be of an imperfect order, the lapse of perfection into imperfection. Alexander reverses the problem, and envisages it as that of showing how the imperfect can form any basis upon which, undirected and blindly, the perfect comes to be. Whilst one may think this is the harder path to take, it cannot be said to be necessarily anti-theistic. Whitehead starts from a deliberate rejection of the idea of an all-powerful creator. So long, he says, as the temporal world is conceived as the self-sufficient completion of a creative act derived from an ultimate principle, the best result we can hope for is the Buddhist nirvana. But this notion of God he traces to Aristotle, plus a prepossession of Christian theology, plus the idea of imperial Caesar; a combination of God the philosophical principle, the personification of moral energy, the imperial ruler of the universe. It does not owe anything to the 'Galilean' strain in Christian thought which dwelt upon the tender elements of the world, of love which realizes itself in the immediacy of a kingdom not of this

The Philosophical Approach to Religion

world. 'If', says Whitehead (*Science and the Modern World*, p. 222), 'we adhere to the idea of God as the metaphysical basis of reality, there can be no alternative but to discern in Him the source of both evil and good.' Or again (p. 237), 'The presentation of God under the aspect of power awakens every modern instinct of critical reaction.' A further passage relates Whitehead's position to Alexander's. 'Religion is the vision of something which stands beyond, behind, and within the passing flux of immediate things; something which is real, yet waiting to be realized; something which is a remote possibility, and yet the greatest of present facts; something that gives meaning to all that passes, and yet eludes apprehension; something whose possession is the final good, and yet is beyond all reach; something which is the final ideal, and the hopeless quest' (*Ibid.*, p. 238).

A philosophical criticism of this type of thought would involve more than can be undertaken here. The purpose of introducing it is not critical; rather is it to indicate that there are other avenues to the idea of God being made by men who are able and sincere thinkers, to whom the traditional theism does not appeal. Yet if God is to be, as Whitehead certainly desires, more than a philosophical principle, the ultimate test of these doctrines will not be in their philosophical soundness, but in their relation to religious experience. Any doctrine of God that is not simply a doctrine of a metaphysical principle, must stand before the bar of religious experience, just as much as any doctrine of the nature of the physical world must be judged by its ability to meet the facts of that world as it is known to us. Our actual experience of God cannot be said naturally to conform to the traditional conception of the world ruler, even though we may persuade ourselves that in some way it does. Will it be better fitted to Whitehead's or Alexander's ways of seeing the problem? That remains to be seen, and with it lies the future of these ideas. But at least we may be glad that, if from other standpoints, and with results that are disturbing to the ways of thought to which most of us have easily accustomed ourselves, these thinkers are approaching the greatest task of human thought, the idea of God, and by breaking ground therein must at least help to give us a fresh realization of the conditions of the ultimate problem of theism.

Chapter IV

The Idea of the Universe

THEISTIC CONCEPTIONS

NEITHER religion nor theism is committed to any particular theory of the nature of the physical universe. Such questions belong rather to science and philosophy, and religion holds but a watching brief in their findings. The questions in which religion is more closely interested will come under review later, when we speak of God and the world, and God and man. There seems no particular reason, for example, to protest against the scientific theories of the universe as expanding, or as 'running down', or even to the ultimate disappearance of man from this planet. Those who accept the reasoning of idealism are quite unperturbed by any such prophecies, because the supremacy of mind makes it certain that mind cannot be put out of existence by any physical happenings, whatever be their character. Altogether, apart from this, if the universe is the workshop of God, in which His purposes are fashioned, its ultimate physical fate cannot affect the carrying out of those purposes, and nothing else matters.

Indirectly, however, the theory we accept as to the nature of the universe, in its metaphysical rather than its physical aspects, will generally have some bearing on our conception of God and man. Yet of the various theories which come under our notice in this chapter, only one, materialism, cannot be a theistic theory, and must necessarily be opposed by theism, since a strict materialism denies the existence of anything that is immaterial and casts all spiritual values out of the universe. Even so, it is conceivable that, with the new conceptions of matter, a new materialism might arise that could be shaped at least into pantheism.

Most philosophic theism professes to be monistic, though like the unity of Trinitarianism, it finds itself in somewhat unstable equilibrium; in this case because of the outward pluralism of life. Popular theism has always been dualistic in its attitude

The Philosophical Approach to Religion

towards good and evil. There is, despite the zeal of monists, no original sin in pluralism that renders it altogether unfitted to be a religious philosophy.

Of the two theories of the relation of mind to matter, realism is dualistic in opposing mind to a non-mental reality also self existent, and though both may be said to be aspects of a transcendent reality, this is little more than a gesture towards monism. Idealism may be pluralistic or monistic, but in its assertion that all reality is mental, it is qualitatively monistic, and approaches unity more closely than realism. The philosophy of religion has a free choice, however, between both theories.

DUALISM

DUALISM was of a religious character before it arose in the philosophical sense. In the teaching of Zoroastrianism the two principles of good and evil, both independent and creative, were held to be in opposition, and man was drawn into the struggle between them. The end was held to be the triumph of good, and on this ground the modern Parsi and some European writers have called the system monotheistic, though what impressed the Greek was its sharply contrasted dualism. Some think that the doctrine of God and the devil in the Old Testament was influenced from Persian sources. At any rate, that doctrine is typical of religious dualism.

In the philosophical sense, we find the dualistic v. monistic controversy in the philosophy of India, where pantheistic monism is the orthodox form, but another system of philosophy —Sānkhya—recognizes the dualism between matter and soul. Amongst the Greeks, the early thinkers were unwittingly dualistic in most cases, and later thinkers, such as Plato, Aristotle, and the Stoics, revealed some dualistic tendency, the reason being that the force of the sharp antithesis between mind and matter was not appreciated in those days. Even the Neoplatonists, to whom dualism was a nightmare, did not conceive a consistent monism. Plotinus was obliged to resort to mysticism to attain it, and was unable to account for the existence of matter, the 'first evil'.

The Idea of the Universe

Philosophical Dualism

Descartes, who was the pioneer of modern philosophy, divided reality into 'extension' and 'thought', a dualism which neither he nor his successors ever reconciled. Spinoza merged both into 'substance' and rigid monism. Locke repeated Descartes' position, and with it the common sense philosophy of the 'plain man', that the world consists in a multitude of finite substances which are material, and our thought which reveals the material world to us. Over all this there is God. Wolff, in Germany, taught the absolute dualism that the outer world and the world of consciousness were entirely distinct, and so fixed the modern use of the word dualism as the theory that regards mind and matter as mutually independent. Kant's division between mind and 'things-in-themselves' was a legacy from Wolff.

The hypothesis of psycho-physical parallelism is an expression of this dualism, though it often goes with the 'double aspect theory, which regards mind and matter as two aspects of something which is both and neither. The ordinary interaction theory is dualistic, and has to face the difficulty that all dualistic theories must meet, of explaining what is the difference between mind and matter, and how two entirely different things can be related and interact.

Dualism may be absolute or relative. The former holds the independent existence of matter and mind; the latter makes them independent of each other but alike dependent on God, which is the common-sense position of the ordinary man. In what will be said subsequently on the subject of idealism, the answer to absolute dualism will be suggested. Relative dualism meets the same objection to the independent existence of matter, together with an added objection that it forms a needless link in the chain of causation, since, if God be the cause of our minds perceiving, there is no need for an independent matter between the cause, God, and its effect upon us.

James Ward pointed out that the real dualism was within experience. It was that of subject and object. But experience is a unity, so that actually a practical solution is found to the problem in the organic unity of our experience. It is a theoretical solution we lack. Yet we are responsible for our own difficulties. We divide what God has joined, and have split up the reality revealed in experience as a unity, into two independent realms, matter and mind. Then we complain that we cannot put them together again. But the difficulty is caused by ourselves treating experience in an artificial way, and then being vexed to find that it does not lend itself to our treatment. Up till modern times, matter was regarded as a non-mental, independent, and extended substance. This view has collapsed through the modern identification of matter with electricity or energy. Consciousness may be thought of as a form of energy, but not of the same type as electrical energy. So the dualism remains. Some modern scientists appear to be rejecting dualism for monism of an idealistic rather than a materialistic type. The difficulties of dualism make monism appear attractive, yet monism presents its own difficulties. Idealism obviates speaking of independent matter and mind, by regarding all reality as mental and matter as a form of thought. Yet even so, it has to explain why matter appears to be other than thought, and still more it has to show what is the relation between human minds and the mind of God. One answer to the latter question leads us to absolute monism, which is close akin to pantheism; another leads to pluralistic idealism, which raises a new type of dualism, that of an independent divine and independent human mind, so that the old problem still raises its head.

MONISM

FROM the difficulties of dualism, it has seemed to many a relief to turn to the simplicity of monism, until closer acquaintance with monistic theories has shown that monism has its own difficulties, quite as formidable as those of dualism. Dualism at least has 'animal faith' behind it. Monism is unknown in experience, and when we come to ask precisely what is meant by this apparently attractive theory, troubles are born and multiply rapidly.

There is more than one type of monism. The belief that reality is of one kind throughout is qualitative monism; the belief that it is one single being is numerical monism. The latter type is almost bound to embrace the former also. But there are qualitative monists who are numerical pluralists, such as the idealists who hold mind is the one reality, but that there are

The Idea of the Universe

many minds and not one all-inclusive Absolute. This is the position of Lotze and the personal idealists. The most uncompromising monist was Spinoza, whose God, or Substance, was the sole reality. Schopenhauer was a monist who identified the Absolute with unconscious will, while Hegel's Absolute was identified with God as pure thought. The term monism was due to Wolff and popularized by Haeckel, whose materialism was a type of qualitative monism. Most theism is avowedly monistic, though popular belief is dualistic in outlook.

A modern theory advocated by Morton Prince and others is that the ultimate reality is an immaterial energy which at a certain point of complexity emerges as consciousness. Body and mind are really the same. Matter represents the way in which we apprehend those other forms of reality which are not ourselves. In ourselves, reality appears as spirit, in the external world as matter. It is the same reality in both cases. It is claimed that this reconciles idealism and materialism and satisfies our demand for monism.

This theory is descriptive but not explanatory. If we stress the word emergence as so many do to-day, we merely call attention to the unexplained appearance of a new factor, but we do not explain anything thereby. Why energy, which is qualitatively one, should take such wholly different forms as matter and consciousness, according to the degree of complexity, this theory does not and cannot say.

The advocates of monism make confident claims that the theory is the only finally satisfactory view of the universe. We are told by a recent writer of repute that if there is to be a Christian philosophy at all, it must be monistic to be complete, and that the religious consciousness makes an imperious demand for unity. Yet no sufficient reason is given for any such assumption. All that can be said is that philosophy cannot be content with dualism, or that, since obviously a dualistic view is not the last imaginable solution, the mind must press towards monism. This, however, is psychological, not logical. It begs the question by assuming that, metaphysically, ultimate reality must conform to our ways of thought. At no time less than the present has this been possible. The small scale phenomena of Nature, as illustrated by modern atomic theories, suggest to us that we may have to admit that the nearer we get to ultimate physical

The Philosophical Approach to Religion

reality, the nearer we get to what is, if not irrational, super-rational. Neither the law of the conservation of energy nor even that of non-contradiction can hold in this sphere in the same sense as it holds ordinarily. All we can say is that we find here that which can be represented mathematically, but we have no right to say more. We cannot find any analogies with the world of the senses, and we cannot even argue that our mathematical symbolization of this unknown characterizes it, any more than an actual existing engine is characterized by the mathematical figures by which its tractive effort is calculated.

From the psychological standpoint, as from the aesthetic, the attractions of monism are manifest, but in the actual world of experience, dualism appears everywhere—good and bad, true and false, mind and matter, living and dead, man and woman, heaven and hell. It is a radically and impenitently dualistic universe in which we live. Monists tell us that this must be reducible to one ultimate source. One may admit what can be said for this. But we cannot demand that reality must in its ultimate nature conform to the demands of our intellects which were built for practical purposes.

However much, then, monism attracts us, we must not allow to it more than it can rightly claim as a theory of the universe. Moreover, even at best there are serious difficulties before it. Numerical monism, if it admits God at all, must be pantheism. Even the milder forms of monism have a pantheistic tinge. Further, we should remember that, despite our talk of it, no monism is ever consistently conceived by us, since we can never actually overcome the subject-object relation within experience. Hence Plotinus was driven to mysticism to attain union with the divine, and, in Christanity and Hinduism alike, a similar path has been followed. Indeed, the inveterate dualism of experience seems responsible for the Hindu doctrine of 'maya' or illusion, by which is explained away the world of sense. Readers of Bradley's *Appearance and Reality* will recollect how utterly uncharacterizable Bradley found the Absolute to be. Again, causal monism, as it is sometimes called, argues that causation implies not an infinite number of independent causes, but one single cause. Much in the same way it is argued that since all our knowledge is relative and what we call a fact is a

The Idea of the Universe

group of relations, there must be behind all an absolute and unrelated reality. This may be, however, the way in which we are obliged to look at facts, rather than a necessary truth. It does not explain the outward and apparent pluralism of life. If it causes an error, then error as well as truth must be part of ultimate reality. If monism is true and pluralism an error, how is it that monism at any rate appears to lose its unity and disintegrate in the manifold?

Historically, monisms have been idealistic or materialistic. Neither reconciles the dualism of experience. They have been aspirations whose appeal has been to the imagination rather than to strict reasoning, and it is not obvious that monism has the better of the argument against pluralism.

Monism and Religion

Religious philosophy may be qualitatively monistic, but unless it is numerically pluralistic it will lapse into pantheism. The best type of monism is *panentheistic*, regarding all things as grounded in God, but not identifying God with all reality. This secures the chief advantages of monism and safeguards the essential being-for-self of human souls who none the less live and move and have their being in God. It allows that all reality is one, namely thought, yet the plurality of thinkers is also real. This is not stringent enough to please the rigid monists, but the only idea we can conceive of unity is that of a diversity in harmony; a single undifferentiated unity passes our understanding.

Pluralism

Pluralism shares with dualism the rejection of the cardinal tenet of monism that the world is in reality one and only in appearance many, but where philosophical dualism resolves itself into an opposition between matter and soul or spirit, pluralism takes various forms and degrees. The most stringent type of pluralism holds that reality is composed of a number of discrete and wholly independent elements. There have been materialistic pluralisms, but the materialism of Haeckel proclaimed itself monistic. The most radical spiritual pluralist was Leibniz, whose philosophy was perhaps not unconnected with

The Philosophical Approach to Religion

his keen interest in the discoveries that resulted from the newly-invented microscope. Leibniz represents a pluralistic realism, though his influence has been felt more in pluralistic idealism, since the realism of Leibniz found no place for matter. All that was existent was a myriad multiplicity of simple self-subsistent spiritual beings, soul-atoms, not atoms of matter, the monads. They are 'metaphysical points', being without parts, but having something vital, and a kind of perception. A material organism is a collection of such monads. The monad possesses neither extension nor shape, it is strictly and literally an atom, because it cannot be subdivided into any parts. Monads are indestructible and differ only in quality and internal action. They are 'windowless', each being unable either to influence or be influenced by any other monad. The soul is the supreme monad of the individual body, and God is the ultimate of all monads. This represents the most severe type of spiritual pluralism. Leibniz, as previously mentioned, accounted for the unity of our experience, by the postulate that by pre-established harmony the internal and independent states of each monad are adjusted to all the rest, and, therefore, though the monads are windowless, they behave as if there were interaction between them all. Moreover, as Leibniz also insisted, each monad represents from its own point of view the whole, meaning that each is a reflection of the whole, as every drop of water might be said to reflect in itself the ocean.

Leibniz represents the most definite type of pluralism because he denied the existence of any interconnecting unity amidst the monads. Each monad was a world in itself, shut in and complete. The consequence is that Leibniz offers a theory of spiritual atoms, regulated by the inner nature given them through the pre-established harmony, instead of material atoms upon which external forces exert an influence. Leibniz was obliged to recognize a unity in the world for which his monads could not account. He admitted such unity existed ideally, existed, that is to say, for the creative mind that planned it, but not as an actual fact of the world of experience. None the less, the fact that God, who, according to Leibniz, because He is God must be thought of as creating the best of possible worlds, made unity by means of the pre-established harmony, implies that such unity is a good, and necessary to this best possible of

The Idea of the Universe

worlds. It seems to follow that the pluralistic universe of monads without such unity cannot be the best, which is a considerable departure from strict pluralism.

In short, strict pluralism, in the end, has to admit the One, just as strict monism has to admit the Many. The position of modern pluralism was well expressed by James, when he said monists declare that surely there must be some connexion between things, and added that the whole question was one of the extent of the 'some'. Pluralism is the doctrine that there is no absolute unity throughout all things as monism insists. The actual world is a mixture of the one and the many, of disjunction and conjunction. Monism admits that it appears as such, but insists that this diversity is apparent, not real. For pluralism this is an unproven dogma, an ideal that appeals to imagination rather than a defensible fact of experience. The issue therefore has become clarified. It amounts to this, that pluralism accepts the multiplicity we find in life as an ultimate fact, whilst for monism the unity also found is the ultimate fact, and the diversity unreal. For pluralism the unity is not unreal but partial.

One of the most interesting examples of a pluralism that possesses many of the characteristics of monism is presented by the late J. E. McTaggart. McTaggart was in some respects the most thorough-going Hegelian in this country, and yet he changed Hegel's monistic Absolute into a society of eternal timeless finite souls, pre-existent as well as immortal. He adopted the Platonic dictum that the number of these souls must always be the same. They are fundamental differentiations of the Absolute, determinate in nature and number, concerning which Pringle-Pattison remarked that it showed a Malthusian anxiety as to the overpopulation of the spiritual world! But McTaggart believed that each of these souls was reincarnate through an infinite number of phases, and as he admitted we have no memory in this life of any previous existences, he had to assume a kind of substrate, like the Buddhist and Hindu 'karma', as the vehicle by which the results of each life were carried forward, and the identity of the individual maintained. This also afforded the necessary unity that made the finite selves a permanent society, but such an underlying unity was not God. The Absolute was a society of such selves in perfect mutual relationship with each other and with the whole. Its unity was simply that of a common fellowship, such as a college affords to the students within it. For such a pluralistic idealism as that of Prof. Howison, God serves as the central monad in the eternal society. For McTaggart's idealism the society is its own unity. McTaggart affords us an example of a pluralism which might be said to assume unity without sufficient reason. The fact which he stresses is the plurality of spirits. Their unity is a mere arbitrary inexplicable chance, without basis or reason. The underlying substrate that serves as a unity is a pure hypothesis, and no single fact of experience attests it. For all we can say, every soul that exists has no link with any previous soul. If we were immortal on earth this type of pluralism might be justified, but as an explanation of this mortal life, it serves no purpose whatever. One cannot say that McTaggart's departure from Hegel in any way strengthened the philosophy they shared in common.

Pluralism is the sequel to the pragmatic theory of knowledge, and as such has been largely concerned with a polemic against absolutism. But pluralism has claims as a constructive religious philosophy of which the chief embodiment is found in Ward's *Realm of Ends*. Ward's starting point was the many as real. He points out that those who start from the one are apt to treat the world as existent simply for the glory of God, whilst those who start from the many are apt to treat God as if He were simply the necessary adjunct of it. Ward believed that the idea of the relation between God and the world as love was the 'via media.' He refused the term pluralist as he considered that his admission of the interaction of minds placed his views outside pluralism, of which he regarded James as more typical. Yet Ward, though he admitted that the one was inexplicably the ground of the many, by his insistence on the reality of the many placed himself amongst the pluralists rather than the strict monists.

It is becoming apparent that the difference between monism and pluralism is in degree more often than in kind. Spinoza represents the most stringent type of monism, Leibniz the most stringent pluralism. The names monist and pluralist have come, however, to denote the degree of approximation to the one or other, rather than two consistently opposed doctrines. If

The Idea of the Universe

any degree of reality is admitted to finite existence, strict monism is compromised; if any recognition is made of a unity underlying the many, strict pluralism is compromised. Most philosophies have made concession in one way or other, and hence the alternative monist or pluralist ceases to be contradictory and becomes merely contrary.

Materialism

Materialism is really nothing but the naive realism of common sense in philosophical garb. It is not surprising, therefore, that it is ancient. The Sānkhyan philosophy of India, though not materialistic in essence, is materialistic in aspect. Democritus and Epicurus taught materialism in Greece, and Mencius attacked a materialism found in China in the third century B.C. With the coming of Christianity, materialism was laid aside, and not destined to revive till the days of Hobbes. Later, La Mettrie and Von Holbach, much more thoroughgoing than Hobbes in the materialistic faith, popularized the doctrine in France, and the French Revolution followed, to stimulate their teaching. Next, it flourished in Germany in the writings of Büchner and others. After Darwin's discoveries, materialism came in as a flood, and Flint, writing in 1877, called it the most prevalent and formidable type of anti-theistic theory. Now it is moribund, not only because the old belief in the actuality and certainty of the existence of matter has gone, but not less because of the intrinsic defects of materialism as a theory professing to account for the universe. Indeed, its triumph in the mid-nineteenth century was perverse, since Darwinism marked a great advance in biology, precisely the sphere where materialism is weakest. The new ideas in biology, the notion of evolution, were bound to make manifest the inadequacy of materialism, though at first neither friend nor foe seemed to realize that fact, and materialism posed as the truly scientific theory of the universe. Yet before the close of that century, the new conceptions of energy and the molecular theories dealt further blows at the old type of materialism. Its discomfiture was completed in the present century by the theory of relativity, which destroyed the idea of a definite present moment at which all matter was simultaneously real. The break-up of materialism as a theory is coincident with the break-up of the classical idea of matter. Haeckel, who fought the rear guard action of materialism, was forced to hylozoism and panpsychism to keep his attempt to equate spirit and energy from collapse.

Looked at from the standpoint of the present, it appears curious that the claims which were made for materialism were taken as seriously as they were. It was claimed to be monistic, but as untold billions of atoms can scarcely be called a satisfactory basis for monism, it was presumed that all were manifestations of a single reality. But on the modern electrical theory of matter, whilst one may call electricity 'real', in no intelligible sense can it be called a single reality such as monism presumes, for as Bertrand Russell has said, electricity is not a thing at all. It is 'a way in which things behave'.

Again, it is evident that materialism employed a circular type of argument when it explained our sensations from the notion of matter which is obtained through the senses. No materialist ever explained what he meant by calling his theory true. Truth is not a property of matter. Our thoughts might conceivably be called chemically correct but on materialistic principles it is meaningless to assert they are logically correct. A materialist may claim his theory is necessitated, but he cannot in any intelligible sense call it true until he has shown us that matter is true, or that truth is a form of matter. The Behaviourists, who have bowed consciousness out of psychology, have not attempted to show that consciousness is a material, but only that it is a superfluous, thing.

It is of no little interest to notice how the notion of the nature of the ultimately real has changed. Science, in its earlier days, dealt with that which could be observed. Then it passed to the stage when what was unobservable, but none the less was thought to be imaginable, occupied its attention. Dalton's atom was supposed to be an infinitely small elastic particle of matter, and when matter was first identified with energy, the illustration of the vortex ring, like the ring of smoke puffed from a cigar, was pressed into service. All this has now gone. We are far from the days when Lord Kelvin could declare that knowledge which could not be expressed by means of a model was meagre and unsatisfactory. Not only does the electron fail

The Idea of the Universe

to behave like the things that our senses apprehend, but it does not accord with our geometrical notions, so that what was once called its radius, is now denoted simply as R. The 'sun and planet' illustration of its relation to the proton or nucleus is no longer regarded as useful, but only as misleading. If we ask for information regarding it, we are presented with a set of mathematical equations, and told that these represent the way it behaves, but what it is that so behaves is not a question for physics. Physics deals with the relations between phenomena, not the phenomena themselves. As Whitehead puts it (*Science and the Modern World*, p. 21): 'The progress of science has now reached a turning point. The stable foundations of physics have broken up.... The old foundations of scientific thought are becoming unintelligible. Time, space, matter, material, ether, electricity, mechanism, organism, configuration, structure, pattern, function, all require reinterpretation.'

Lord Balfour once said we knew too much about matter to be materialists any longer. It would be more apt, to-day, to say we know too little. Matter has melted into mathematics, and in a sense Pythagoras's saying has become true that the essence of all things is number. As Mather said, matter consists of tiny particles of nothing moving very swiftly. It is ironical that materialism, which so confidently claimed the friendship and alliance of 'science' has been wounded to death in the house of its friends.

It is sometimes said that since matter is a form of energy, we may assume that energy and mind are two aspects of one reality. We certainly may, but it is an assumption, and there is nothing in the modern scientific analysis of matter to warrant it. Matter as an existing fact known to the senses was the basis of materialism, and now that matter can be called 'tiny particles of nothing', the materialist has no longer the shelter of common sense belief in matter as an auxiliary to his philosophy. None the less, the fact that matter has thus vanished, whilst destructive to materialism, is no ground for asserting that matter has been shown to be a form of spiritual reality, or that matter, whatever it may be, and mind, are twin sides of one fact. Such a position is arguable on the ground of philosophy, but the scientific analysis of matter has nothing to tell us of what may be its ultimate nature. It merely declares that a mathematical expression of its behaviour serves the purpose of physics better than the old idea of matter as an extended mass of invisible atoms.

Though scotched, it does not follow that materialism is killed. There are plenty of practical materialists, and plenty who are unwilling to admit the spiritual elements of experience, and so long as these remain, and philosophies continue to be expressions of life rather than of thought, will there be the possibility of a phoenix-like resurrection of materialism from the ashes into which it is now dissolved.

Realism and Idealism

The recent scientific discoveries as to the nature of matter and the constitution of the universe have aroused anew the old conflict of realism and idealism. The ordinary man never doubts the reality of the material universe. Our language is, as Bergson said, a language of solids. We refer to an important thing as 'material' or 'substantial', and say that it 'matters'. We use words like impression, aspiration, subject, sentiment, feeling, and many others in referring to mental processes, though all originally had a material significance. The word for soul or spirit and the word for breath or wind are interchangeable in most languages. If we want to express the roots (another material term) of the discussion (yet another) we speak of 'getting down to brass tacks'. Santayana speaks of 'animal faith', and the animal faith of the natural man never doubts the reality and abiding quality of the objects of his senses The issue of realism versus idealism is one of the last two centuries. Parmenides, about 500 years before Christ, said that thought and the object of thought were one, but this remained an isolated suggestion. Despite his spiritual conception of reality, Plato was a realist, and Aristotle never doubted the eternity of 'hylē'. In the fourteenth century, a little-known schoolman, Nicholas of Autrecourt, gained a glimpse of the doctrine of idealism, but the modern phase began with the sharp distinction between 'extension', virtually matter, and 'thought' in Descartes' system. Though a realist, Leibniz, as we have said, took the discussion a step nearer to idealism by abandoning belief in the reality of matter. It was Berkeley (1684–1753) who demonstrated the slender foundations of the popular belief in a world that existed

The Idea of the Universe

independently of perception. It is, of course, true that long before Hindu philosophers had taught that the external world was 'maya' or illusion. This, however, was imparted as an esoteric mystery, and substantiated not by philosophical analysis, but by similes, for example by saying that as a man walking upon a path sees what he thinks is a snake, and turns aside, whereas actually the object is a coil of rope, so he sees what he thinks is a real world, but actually its nature is maya. Berkeley did not treat the existing world as an illusion, but he pointed out that it depended for its existence on being present to mind. Yet as mind included the mind of God as well as that of man, Berkeley admitted the reality of the universe, not as existing for itself, but only for the mind of God.

The doctrine of idealism is somewhat difficult for those who are not familiar with philosophical questions to grasp, and it will therefore be better to set it out in detail.

Let us start with the words, 'Roses have thorns.' They also have scent and colour. We think that if every mind, both animal and human, were non-existent, there would still be the same material world, and roses would continue to 'waste their sweetness on the desert air', and their brilliant colour also. We should not say their thorns continue to scratch, for thorns, we imagine, scratch only when someone touches them. Yet it is as exactly as true to say roses smell when someone smells them, and are coloured when someone sees them.

There is no doubt, therefore, that two factors enter into perception; the 'things' perceived, the mind perceiving. Under what conditions, then, does the mind perceive? It perceives the scent of the rose, but scent is caused by minute material particles which touch the membrane of the nose. Yet those particles are not scent. Nor is the scent something in the nose, much less something in the rose. It is a process in the brain by which the mind perceives. We localize the scent in the rose, the scratch we localize in the finger, not in the thorn, but both are alike brain-processes [1] which mind has perceived. So with the other senses. Colour we speak of as belonging to the coloured object, though it is due to wave-lengths, longer or shorter, being refracted by objects. Yet a wave-length of light is not a colour. When the light goes colour goes; alter the light and colour

[1] See preface, p. 10.

The Philosophical Approach to Religion

alters. Colour, then, does not belong to the object perceived, but to the perceiving mind. So with sound. It is caused by vibrations. A deaf man may *feel* an organ playing, but cannot *hear* it because the ears do not set up in the brain the process which yields sound. Heat is also due to vibration; taste to the stimulation of palate and tongue by a dissolving substance; but all the senses are alike. What they refer to is not something belonging, to the object perceived, but to the perceiving mind. Moreover, 'all perception is illusion', as Lotze put it, for we always perceive more than is given

This was recognized by Locke, who proposed accordingly to admit that these 'secondary' qualities were not in the objects, but in our minds, and that objects merely had power to produce them in us. He added that the power to produce a sensation was not the same as objects themselves. They seem differently constituted. Colour changes with light, but not so hardness. We can conceive of a colourless object as a blind man must do, but not of an untouchable one. But as Berkeley saw, this makes no difference. We know primary qualities just as we know secondary, by sensation, and sensation belongs to the mind, not to the object.

This does not imply that the only things which exist are minds and their objects, and all that can be said of such objects is that they are something which arouses sensations. There exist also relations between objects, relations of space, time, likeness and unlikeness, degree, &c. Yet these relations do not belong to the objects, but to the mind that compares them. For example, if there is two feet of space between X and Y the space is not *in* X or in Y. We say it is between them, which means that it exists only for a mind that can grasp X and Y and their relations. Similarly with the other relations.

We see then, that, on investigation, sensations and relations perceived by mind make up what we call the external world. Matter which we think of commonly as something solid and substantial in itself, disappears into groups of sensations. Our own body exists for us only because of the sensations it transmits to the mind; so the body, and the material brain it contains, are in this respect the same as any other kind of matter, known by mind, and not as independent of it. We have spoken

The Idea of the Universe

as if sensations existed independently, but since the body which transmits them to the mind does not, neither do they. Matter then seems to depend for its existence on mind.

It may be objected 'Science teaches the reality of matter.' Such a statement has little point. Strictly speaking, science is concerned only with the properties of matter. It was once thought that matter was permanently extended substance, although probably all matter was ultimately of one kind. But instead of imagining ultimate indivisible atoms as the basis of matter, positive and negative electrical charges now appear as the bricks of the universe. Even science, then, turns the solid world, that seems so evidently real, into electricity. But electricity is known only by mind that perceives it. The world and the fulness thereof may be resolved into electricity, but electricity at the last resort is to be defined only as something perceived by the mind.

Others advance an objection much more to the point, namely that science implies that matter existed before mind, and the universe before man. We might reply that this objection implies absolute time, and all statements of time are relative to the observer. Apart, however, from this, we might accept the objection as it stands and reply that when we speak of mind we include more than human minds. The world existed for the Creator's mind. Indeed, Dr. Rashdall based an argument for the existence of a Divine Mind upon this very fact.

The strength of all these objections is at heart the difficulty of believing that matter can be dependent on mind. Yet my mind can produce from its imagination a picture that has all the characteristics of actual perception. In a dream, a whole material world depends on and is called forth by my mind, and whilst the dream lasts it has all the marks of reality. Of course, this is reproduction, but, none the less, in it matter depends on mind. Again, if I 'see stars' because of a blow, or hear buzzing because of deafness, my mind is producing material effects without the ordinary material cause. Moreover, in cases of 'imaginary disease', or the 'stigmata' of St. Francis, the mind directly achieves material results. It may be objected that all these cases might be explained by a dualism of mind acting on independent matter. None the less, matter is known only because the mind *thinks* it. To insist that it does somehow exist independently of mind does not alter the fact that it is mind which thinks of it existing thus. Moreover, in saying matter wholly depends on mind, we include the divine mind as well as human mind.

The celebrated saying of Hume that the arguments for idealism admitted of no refutation, yet carried no conviction, explains more than anything else the reluctance of many thinkers to accept them. Yet after all, it is a sheer appeal to animal faith and common sense prejudice. What is irrefutable should convince, and the weight of reasoning is with idealism, though the natural attitude of our minds is towards realism. But there is nothing advanced by the idealist that offends those moral spiritual and aesthetic intuitions which do at times rebel against what seems plausible from a purely argumentative point of view. Under these circumstances, there seems nothing beyond blind trust in our untrustworthy senses to give any answer from the other side of our nature to the reasoning in favour of idealism.

To sum up, if the idealist is right, the poet was wrong in saying that full many a flower was born to waste its sweetness on the desert air, for what does not exist for mind cannot be shown to exist at all. Berkeley defined the essence of matter in the words 'Esse est percipi', to be is to be perceived. As this suggests sense perception merely, whereas sense perception is far from being the whole content of our minds, the saying would have been clearer as 'Esse est intellegi', to be is to be thought. The realist cannot maintain that he can *think* of things that must exist even when such existence is un-thought-of. The usual way of meeting the difficulty from the realist side is to denounce Berkeley's position as 'the ego-centric predicament', which simply means that we can no more think of reality apart from our thought of it than we can leap from our own shadow. But it is urged that this need not mean that reality is identical with our thought, only that it is invariably and inevitably connected with it. Whilst we must admit from the nature of the case that we cannot think of reality apart from our relation to it, we must not assume that it exists only in that relation, just as we must assume under similar conditions, if we believe in God, that He exists apart from our relation to Him.

The reply is that the two cases are not analogous. We cannot

The Idea of the Universe

have any knowledge of matter apart from mind, nor show how mind can be produced from matter. But mind is a self existent reality in our experience: in Descartes' phrase, 'Cogito ergo sum.' Descartes discovered he could doubt everything except that he doubted. We are not obliged to give to matter the independent existence we are obliged to give to God as mind. Matter we can think away, but never mind, and that is why we are justified in assuming that mind has a being for self that matter need not be thought to possess. That, as regards matter, to be is to be thought of may or may not be held to be proved, but it cannot be held to be disproved. Dr. Rashdall has put the question in a nutshell from the standpoint of relations. 'Apart from mind there can be no relatedness; apart from relatedness no space; apart from space no matter. It follows that apart from mind there can be no matter' (*Philosophy and Religion*, p. 11).

If matter, then, depend for its existence on mind, are we to assume that when it is perceived or thought of by no mind, it goes out of existence; that, for example, my lecture room comes into and goes out of existence throughout the day according as there is or is not any one perceiving it or thinking of it? Does not such a supposition render idealism farcical? It will, of course, be remembered that whether any human mind perceives it or not, the material world must be thought to exist for the creative mind upon which it depends, and by reason of which it exists. As far, however, as I am concerned, it is true to say that the existence of my room when it is not an object of thought is possible rather than actual from the theoretical standpoint, though, from the practical standpoint, we seldom need to distinguish the two.

In my absence, then, it exists as a possibility (incidentally a very strong possibility), but except in so far some mind envisages it, it does not exist *actually*, though indeed the possibility seems as certain as the actuality in this case. But if I lived in a land where whole houses disappeared at once by cyclone or earthquake it might not seem so. The external world then, according to idealism, is an order of actual and possible sensations, existing for minds. The possible, because of the regularity of experience, seem to us as certain often as the actual, and so there grows up the indefensible notion of a world independently

The Philosophical Approach to Religion

existing, but there are no such things as sensations apart from mind, and the whole evidence we have of an external world comes from sensation. There is no point in speaking of the external world as independently existing of itself. The external world is the totality of actual and possible groups of sensation (i.e. sensations and relations which bind or group them together); any object is a single group; a law of nature the constant relation existing between these groups.

The terms matter or external world, then, represent, for idealism, names for the objects of experience treated apart from the relation they necessarily bear to mind, but just as we ascribe the colour to the object though we recognize that a change in the lighting can instantly change the colour, so the idealist speaking of matter does so without implying that it is independent of mind, even when treated as such. Realism, on the other hand, teaches that things are experienced independently without owing their being or their nature to the fact that they are so experienced by mind.

Our primary reality, then, is our own mind. To ask where our minds are is to assume that minds exist in space, but since space exists only for minds, the question is contradictory. Idealism, however, must face the question of the existence of minds other than that of the individual, or else lapse into solipsism, that is to say the assertion that the only reality is the single observer's mind. But as the following words of McDougall show, solipsism is not the concern of idealism alone. Every form of philosophy must escape solipsism by the same method. As McDougall puts it: 'We affirm that each of us can escape from solipsism only by an act of faith or will that posits a real world of which he is a member. This real world appears to each of us in the form of the phenomena of sense perception; but if he is not to remain a solipsist he must affirm and believe that these appearances are not created by himself, but are rather due to influences or existences, not himself yet affecting him. Or in other words he must believe in the validity of the category of causation; for only by believing that his perceptions are caused by some influence, some real being other than himself, can he escape from solipsism. Let him conceive these influences or existences how he will, the psychological problem still confronts him, and clamours for an answer (*Body and Mind*, p. 180).

The Idea of the Universe

Since our own experience and our own minds are inexplicable apart from the assumption that other minds exist, idealism can recognize that there is a plurality of minds, each existing in its own right. But by itself this is not enough. It can be urged that the *same* idea cannot be in two different minds, and that on idealist principles no two minds can share a common experience. It may be replied that the difficulty is not peculiar to idealism. If, as realism insists, there is a non-mental reality which is perceived by minds, this does not explain why minds should perceive it alike. If two persons look at the same object, to say it is the same object does not alter the fact that two different mental processes are involved by two independent observers seeing it. But why should these two have similar perceptions registered by two utterly independent mental processes? Whether we are realists or idealists, we must assume that there is some similarity in the working of independent mental processes, for even if it be urged that both see the 'same' thing, the question remains why both should see it as the same, just as much as the fact that there are two watches both going does not guarantee that both will keep the same time. Unless there is some harmony between the working of the various minds that perceive, the universe becomes a multiverse, and a common experience an insoluble enigma. There are various ways of meeting the point, but for most idealists, the creative mind represents the common link between the minds it has created, and is held to be in some sense immanent in them.

Apart altogether from idealism, the naive realist who clings to his belief that somehow the external world is what it seems to be, gets cold comfort nowadays from the science which he used to think was his ally. Those who have read the works of Professor Eddington or Sir James Jeans will have found that these writers incline to an idealistic view, from the standpoint of their scientific beliefs. Matter has ceased to be a thing composed of ultimate material atoms for modern science. It becomes a form of energy, that is to say electricity, and whatever electricity is, it cannot be called a material thing. All that we can learn from science is that it is 'the phenomenal manifestation of an unknown something.' This raises one more question. Is idealism forced to assume that minds create what they perceive, or can it admit that there is something other than the perceptions of mind? The answer may be given in Kant's words 'The intellect makes Nature though it does not create it.' This agrees with the notion of an 'Unknown Something'. It is true that we assume but cannot prove it does, we believe in it as an act of faith. But if we do not admit of the existence of anything but our minds, we find it difficult to account for minds being roused into consciousness at all. Hence we come back to our starting point and believe in minds that perceive, and not objects that independently exist and *are perceived*—that is impossible—but in something that independently exists and *causes* mind to perceive. The last question will be to say what this something may be held to be. If we are thorough idealists we shall call it mind too, but some who will agree with our exposition so far do not accept this last contention.

The last question, then, is what is it that lies behind the phenomena our senses organize but do not originate? In philosophical language what are 'noumena' behind 'phenomena'? Three possibilities exist. Reality may be non-mental, mental, or something that is both or neither, some 'tertium quid'.

To look upon matter as a form of electricity may be correct for physics, but we saw that it does not escape the criticism of idealism. Our modern realists ('neo-realists') speak of groups of 'sense-data' as existing independently of mind. Yet this is only a refinement of the older materialism. Its basis is simply and solely the common-sense belief in the existence of actual things, dressed up in philosophical garments. J. S. Mill called matter 'the permanent possibility of sensations', and the expedient of 'sense-data' is little more than this.

To speak of sense-data avoids the contradictions involved in imagining things exist in themselves as we perceive them, but does not avoid the main criticism of idealism. Nor can it explain how mind came into being, but mind can be used to explain how matter comes to exist. Spinoza, Herbert Spencer, and even the materialist Haeckel, admitted the superiority of mind as an explanation of matter, over matter as an explanation of mind.

Others, however, speak of sense-data and mind as independently, existing manifestations of something which is neither, and this is the favourite resource of modern realism. Both mind

The Idea of the Universe

and matter, or rather sense-data, are manifestations of something else. But like Herbert Spencer's Unknowable, this something else is a supposition, for we can argue only by analogy, and here nothing of any analogy can hold. Why then import the unknown and unknowable? It cannot explain the known, and is useless, when the known, mind, will serve our purpose. We may take, therefore, the something that works upon our minds as mind also. How are we to interpret this mind is a disputed question. Theists believe we must interpret it as corresponding to the highest type of mind we know; free, conscious, purposive will. If so, we shall regard the universe as God's will objectified, our experience of it as the effect of God's mind working on our mind. We see, hear, feel as God's will makes us see, hear, feel; but since God's will works regularly and permanently, it appears to us as if embodied in an outward, visible, audible, tangible reality—the external world. Actually, however, all is mind, noumena, and phenomena; things and things-in-themselves, or whatever else they are called. Mind is all, and all is mind.

There have been many types of idealism. Berkeley was, as all pioneers must need be, imperfect in his statement of the implications of the discovery he made. Kant supplied one omission of Berkeley when he showed that mind supplies the relations within which it perceives objects, but Kant ended with a dualism of the *Ding an sich* (thing-in-itself) and its appearances to our minds, between noumena and phenomena, that is to say. Hegel reduced all to mind, but regarded that mind as the Absolute, so that human minds had an adjectival existence as expressions of the Absolute, a position represented in this country in various ways, especially in the philosophies of Bradley and Bosanquet. McTaggart held to a pluralistic idealism. Here, we have expounded the type known as personal idealism, which holds that human minds have a substantival existence, and are not phases of an absolute mind, though they depend for their existence on its creative act and immanent indwelling.

For personal idealism the ultimate reality is made up of centres of experience (monads), and the supreme mind. In this existence we monads are mind-matter centres. The two are never actually divorced, but for explanatory purposes we interpret matter as a form of mind. We can conceive of the non-

The Philosophical Approach to Religion

existence of matter, but never of the non-existence of mind. If we think of the universe as existing apart from any mind, this very fact that our mind is thinking it, shews that we cannot conceive the non-existence of mind. It reveals itself thus to us as immortal and eternal.

Idealism holds that between ourselves and the universe 'spirit speaks to spirit'. It is our minds that know matter and discover the secrets of the material universe. It is far easier to conceive how this is possible if we hold that the material universe is, at last resort, mind also. If so, then in its knowledge of matter our mind is not dealing with an alien substance, but with that which is kin to itself. This affords the best approach to that intricate interaction between the two, which constitutes experience.

It has seemed necessary to devote attention to the exposition of idealism as the point of view from which this book is written. Idealism played a noteworthy part in rebutting the triumphant materialism of the nineteenth century, but since the coming of the twentieth, the turn of the tide has been towards realism. It seems, in view of the new discoveries in physics, that idealism is likely to revive in the future.

It has not been possible to do justice to realist criticisms of idealism. That competent thinkers support both schools shows that there is a case for both, and the basis of realism lies in the conviction that none can ever entirely shake, that our minds do introduce us to a non-mental reality, and that if with idealism we explain this as ultimately mind also, its great difference from all we know as mental, makes that theory seem unlikely. Realism must admit the truth of the idealist position that we have no knowledge of this reality other than through the way our minds present it to us, and that, therefore, to insist that it must be in itself what it appears to us, is as false as to assume that our fellow men must be in themselves what we think them to be, and no other. But realism demurs that though matter is known only to mind, it does not follow that matter exists only for mind, and there, the idealist may concede, is the strong point of realism. But since realism has to agree that this existence cannot be shown to bear any resemblance to the characteristics which we perceive through our minds, there is no support for the commonsense view of an independent reality which exists as we see it. In short, the issue between realism and idealism narrows down

The Idea of the Universe

to the final point that the one teaches that our minds perceive an independent and non-mental reality, and the other teaches that this independent reality can be characterized as a form of mind, and there we must leave the whole question.

Chapter V

The Idea of Man

THE MORAL NATURE OF MAN

IT would be difficult to find any conception whatsoever of the character of human nature that could not be supported by teaching given in some religious system. Those accustomed to the backgrounds of Christian theology are inclined to a distinction in theory between human nature as regenerate and unregenerate—which is sometimes difficult to substantiate fully in practice! But the notion of the natural goodness of mankind was accepted in China many centuries before the Christian era, for the teaching of Confucius that man was born good and equal by nature, but became differentiated by practice, was by no means his own invention. Similarly, to the Stoic, human nature was necessarily made perfect because it was the work of divine perfection which could not bring about anything that was in its essence evil.

The rhetorical confession of the psalmist that he was shapen in iniquity and conceived in sin was made much of by both Jewish and Christian theology, though the Genesis account of man made in the image of God had to be considered, and was met by alleging that this likeness was defaced by the Fall in all the race of Adam. None the less, we find Ecclesiastes saying that God made man upright. It was upon this that Ruskin made the comment, 'You have had false prophets among you who have told you that all men are nothing but fiends and wolves—half beast, half devil. Believe that and indeed you may sink to that. But refuse that, and have faith that God made you upright, though you have sought out many inventions; so will you strive daily to become what your Maker meant and means you to be' (*Crown of Wild Olive*, Lect. III).

The Pelagians, duly condemned in the 39 Articles, maintained that man was good because God, his Maker, was good, that his evil was the result of his own free will, but that no natural impulse was wrong in itself. This involved the denial of original

The Idea of Man

sin and of the belief that physical death was the consequence of sin. In all this, Pelagianism has, despite its condemnation by orthodoxy, triumphed in the Protestant Churches, most of which would also accept the contention that infant baptism was not for the remission of sins. So far, the Pelagian theology was nearer to the truth than the Augustinian, but the contention that some men have been morally perfect and that such a result could be produced either by the law or the gospel, explains why Pelagianism lost its battle. The more sombre views of Augustine prevailed, deepened for Protestantism by the rigour of Calvinism, despite the protests of Rousseau and the 'Back to Nature' school. In the Roman Church, the Jansenists and Pascal worked towards the same ideas in this respect as Calvin and Jonathan Edwards in Protestantism, and the seventh chapter of the Epistle to the Romans became accepted as the psychology of unregenerate human nature. The notion of classical writers, who, like Homer, were inclined to regard sin as a kind of mental lapse, or else as a nemesis that awaits all men, was definitely lost in the dogmatic theology of total depravity. The dogma of depravity gained powerful, though unintentional, support from the unlikely source of Hobbes's writings, but Hobbes's views of human nature as essentially selfish undoubtedly strengthened, on the philosophical side, the theological prepossession of depravity, and actually, if we are to choose between the ideas of human nature which the writings of Hobbes and Rousseau represent, Hobbes comes nearer to truth, even though he is far from being at its centre.

The views that man is good or that he is bad, by nature, are contrary rather than contradictory, and though both are, in their strict forms, untrue, there is enough in human nature to support either. At the root of human behaviour lies an unmoral, but not an immoral, basis, in the instinctive tendencies. Man is neither moral nor immoral by endowment, but only by reason of his ability voluntarily to express his instinctive tendencies in social or in unsocial ways. Excess of any instinctive activity is generally harmful, and there is no doubt that some, by temperament and by responsiveness to environment, are more prone to excess than others. But that is not 'original sin'.

The term 'original sin' is, strictly speaking, inaccurate. It should be original guilt, since a tendency to sin does not become

The Philosophical Approach to Religion

sin until it issues in act. But the idea of the inheritance of guilt has lost its former foundation in the notion of the wrongdoing of the first pair being entailed upon their descendants. Even if it were possible to argue this were still to be accepted, the doctrine assumes the inheritance of an acquired characteristic of a mental order, which is more than doubtful biologically. The difficulties of maintaining the old dogma are therefore not only religious but scientific. Yet it may be taken as almost axiomatic that no widely accepted doctrine that has stood for many years is entirely baseless. What gives meaning to the idea of original sin is the solidarity of the race, the interdependence of us all. None lives to himself, and the individual can never break away utterly from his ancestry and social environment. Moreover, there is a strain of the past in the mental inheritance of us all, and there are moral as well as physical reversions to type in the most cultivated lives. The words 'total depravity' are seldom heard now, but they really were an exaggeration of a perfectly true fact. The human soul is in much the same position as a colony in some continent where the savage aborigines, shut up in the interior, at times burst in upon civilization with fire and sword. It is precisely those mutinies in the soul, even in the best ordered lives, which give the impression that human nature is unregenerate. The old dogma has lost its appeal, but it has not lost all touch with fact, and if choice were necessarily between it and the notions of some sentimental humanitarians, it is likely still to be the extreme nearer to the mean.

The Relation of the Individual to Society

Few things can be more obvious than that an individual is inconceivable apart from the society which bred and fed him, physically and mentally, for mind even more than body depends upon environment for its growth. It is said that those who have been kept in strictly solitary confinement invariably lose their reason after a few years at most. Man's social nature is the result of his inborn characteristics, and in no sense an artificial arrangement forced on him by the conditions of his life on earth.

Yet it is equally true that society is meaningless apart from the individuals who compose it. Loose talk about the 'social consciousness' often seems to suggest that it is an entity in itself, and indeed some writers have gone so far as to treat it as

The Idea of Man

such. In a recent book one meets such a sentence as this: 'The Christian community is something more than its members, and it exists apart from them,' which is exactly as if one wrote, 'The swarm is something more than the bees, and exists apart from them.' What is meant by such unguarded expressions is that society is not the aggregate of its individuals. Logic, as well as sociology, bans this proceeding from the individual to the collective. A sandheap is the aggregate of the grains of sand, and yet even a sandheap as a heap has 'properties that the individual grains as grains do not possess. The better metaphor is that of the chain, which by virtue of its interlinking can do what the individual link cannot do, that is, bend, and reach. A group will act for ends which as individuals they would ignore. Hence it is fully legitimate to speak of special properties of the social consciousness which the individual consciousness does not possess, but that is not to assert its existence apart from individuals.

Civilization is a matter of social integration, and the moral life is a social life. Robinson Crusoe, on his island, might retain some of the morality he had learned in civilization, but had he been born and brought up on his island, nourished, shall we say, by a robot, he could not possibly be thought to have developed a moral sense. It is conceivable, however, that if a number of others, similarly brought up, were placed together, they would develop, in the presence of each other, something of the social nature that they had not learned.

The dependence of every man on the society in which he is brought up makes it impossible to estimate any character without reference to its times, for we all reflect to a greater or larger degree the ideals and conscience of our age. Both the perfection and the imperfection of society and the individual go hand in hand. Yet the greatest men have lived beyond the intellectual and moral limit-lines of their age. 'Our citizenship is in heaven,' and at one and the same time life can be in our own age and yet ahead of it in an ideal 'communion of saints'. Those who have best realized this higher fellowship have lived in the future and the present at the same time. The supreme example of this is given in the life of Jesus.

Individuality is a fact of God, who makes individuals. It is man who creates classes. Individuality may be likened to a biological variation or mutation, a definitely given new factor.

The Philosophical Approach to Religion

It is possible that the environment may stimulate variability, and that it may also have much to do in deciding what variations survive, but there is no reason to assume that it creates the individual, or that he is but the complex of his race. Society itself is unprogressive apart from the initiative of individual members. No one has succeeded in showing how change comes in any society apart from the fact that certain individuals react in a manner different from that which is traditional in the society, and that some of their experiments survive, and become adopted by the society, a process that is true of primitive and developed social orders alike. It is impossible to think that the history of mankind could have been written as it is, apart from some of the outstanding individuals of history. Every fresh orientation of society reveals the individual genius behind it. The relation, therefore, of society to the individual is one of interaction, and in this relation egoism and altruism must find their balance. If egoism is based on inborn self-preserving and acquisitive tendencies, altruism may also find an inborn basis in the parental and group sense, and in the social emotion of sympathy. Altruism may demand that we abate our selfishness, but it can never be selflessness. True altruism is a form of self-realization, and the true egoism is to find one's self in something greater than self. Self-sacrifice may be needful to us, because it balances the tendency to self-assertion, but to speak of God 'sacrificing' Himself is as misleading as to speak of Him pleasing Himself. In a perfect life there is neither egoism nor altruism, for the individual and the common good are one. In all human lives the two must at times seem to conflict, and yet the realization of the unity of individual and society forbids us to think that the two can be on the long-range view in any way hostile. But this is where our faith goes further than our sight.

The Personality and Freedom of Man

The conception of man in relation to God will be found in all religions to be inextricably bound up with the attitude taken towards man's freedom of will and action. Determinism is often treated as if it were purely an attitude adopted by certain scientists, which must be opposed in the interests of religion. Yet religious determinism is older by far than the determinism set forth in the name of science. Indeed, the beginnings of

The Idea of Man

determinism lay in an exaggerated idea of God's omnipotence, which left no room for any true human agency, and the determinism of Islam to-day is precisely of this type. So was the determinism of Calvin, and that of his most ardent disciple, Jonathan Edwards, who was utterly convinced that apart from determinism there could be no morality. On the other hand, the ordinary man, apart from scientific or theological prepossessions, has agreed with Dr. Johnson, 'Sir, we know the will is free, and there's an end on't.' Centuries of discussion have not carried the matter much further, though within recent times there has been a new method of approach to the question, and a new explanation of its apparent insolubility.

The notion that freedom means that any course of action is as likely as any other, is so far from what any libertarian maintains that one can but agree with William James who said that those who want to argue the point on that basis must be put outside till they learn what they are talking about! The real argument is, of course, that the strongest motive must prevail, and that it does so is indicated by the fact that the better we know a character the more confidently can we predict its actions. No libertarian denies that this is so. The psychology of habit makes it evident. But James points out that we can suspend even the most regular habits, and that this indicates free decision against the weight of custom and interest. Bergson indeed denies that we can be said to predict, only to guess, any future action, because the maxim of causation that the same cause always produces the same effect cannot be fulfilled as regards mental causes. The memory of the previous occasions is added to each fresh one and in consequence every mental state is unique, that is to say, unlike any of its predecessors, and the unique must be the unpredictable. The logic of the argument is with Bergson, but a dialectical victory never carries any issue very far.

William James divided determinists into 'hard' and 'soft' varieties. The former treat man as purely a machine. The latter try to get the best of both worlds, of freedom and determinism, by saying that we are 'self-determined'. We act according as we willed, and none but ourselves willed the act, hence it is our own, and we are responsible. The point, however, is whether my self which determines my acts is free or not in so doing. The reply is that actions spring from character, but whence comes character? If it is simply the sum total of the inherited, instinctive and necessarily acquired reactions of my life, then 'I' had nothing to do with the creation of 'Me'. My actions are my own, but in the same sense as my body is my own. I am not responsible for my eye and hair colouring, though they are mine and no one else's. Unless my actions are my own in some sense different from this, it is mere confusion of words to say that I am self-determined.

Others seem to think that, as our actions are not subject to external compulsion, we can be called free, even though every action is, in theory at least, predictable. Mr. Bertrand Russell, for example, denies that the (theoretical) ability to predict the future actions of a man involves the conclusion that they are determined. Our memory of the past did not determine the past, and the only difference is that 'we do not happen to have a memory of the future', a remark which in a manner characteristic of Mr. Russell, conceals the falsity of its analogy by its cleverness. The 'memory of the future,' if we did possess it, would bear no analogy to the memory of what is past, because what has not come into being *ipso facto* has psychological characteristics different from what has happened. All such arguments are attempts to maintain determinism and deny that it involves that we are mere machines. The hard determinist is far more consistent.

The real strength of determinism lies in the supposed analogies from physical science, and its attraction in the belief that without it there can be no scientific study of man. Indeed, some have said with the utmost naiveté that if there is no determinism, psychology cannot be a science, and seemed to regard this as an argument. It is exactly the same temper as that of the mediaeval theologians who held that whatever could not be conformed to the existing dogmas of the Church could not exist, since God was supposed to have revealed the dogmas, and presumably He decided what existed! In the nineteenth century, determinism was triumphant, loudly proclaiming the approval of 'Science', science with a capital S, for its dogmas, and served as a useful handmaid to materialism. James Ward was bold enough to challenge the assumption even in the days of its strength, by asking whether natural laws might not possibly be analogous to the fixed habits of a free activity, which, because they are

The Idea of Man

regular, appear to be unalterable, a thought that reappeared in Bergson's idea of creative evolution. But the collapse of the classical physics through modern research into the structure of the atom, the conception of relativity, and the quantum theory, have altered the scientific attitude to determinism. Heisenberg's principle of indeterminacy states that we cannot predict in any exact sense both the position and the velocity of a particle. The more accurately we determine the one, the less accurately can we determine the other. Hence Eddington remarks, 'Science thereby withdraws its moral opposition to free will. Those who maintain a deterministic theory of mental activity must do so as the outcome of their study of the mind itself, and not with the idea that they are thereby making it more conformable with our experimental knowledge of the laws of inorganic nature' (*Nature of the Physical World*, p. 295). 'Modern physics is drifting away from the postulate that the future is predetermined, ignoring it rather than deliberately rejecting it' (*Ibid.*, p. 306). In the same way Jeans says that science 'has no longer any unanswerable arguments to bring against our innate conviction of free will' (*Mysterious Universe*, p. 29). He adds that the majority of physicists still expect that the old law of causation will somehow be rehabilitated. Others admit the indeterminacy of small scale phenomena, but deny that this bears upon the question. An insurance company can form accurate forecasts upon the length of life amongst its clients whilst knowing nothing about the chances of each individual. In the same way the indeterminacy of the electron cancels out in the mass. This is not the older type of determinism, though it affords a practical argument, but in any case the general appeal to rigid unalterable determinism throughout Nature can no longer avail. The radical objection to determinism, however, is not of this type. It is that any analogy from the physical to the psychical is a false analogy. A person making up his mind represents a unique situation, and one that cannot be paralleled in the sphere of physical causation. If we confined our attention to the psychological characteristics of deliberation and will, we should never imagine that anything analogous to physical causation were taking place. Determinism learns of causation in the physical sphere, and extends it to the mental, ignoring the radical differences between the two.

The Philosophical Approach to Religion

Every mental process is the successor of preceding mental processes, continuous with and relative to them. But this relation bears no analogy to the relation between a physical state and its antecedents. It is possible to connect certain activities of the ductless glands with certain mental states. It is also possible to speak of such a thing as a beautiful sight being the cause of a pleasurable feeling in the beholder. But if any one thinks that there is anything but a verbal analogy between these things and what we mean by physical causation, such as the production of steam by heat, the question is manifestly begged. When we speak of causes in the physical world we have a measurement that will show the balancing of cause and effect, and the certainty that the same cause will produce the same effect. It is absurd to suggest that this holds in the mental sphere, and to speak of mental causation on a par with physical is sheer abuse of terminology, and in every way misleading.

The falsity of the analogy upon which determinism is built is further indicated by the question-begging character of the term 'strongest' motive. There is no meaning in saying that action is determined by it, indeed the very word strong is only metaphorically applicable to motives. If we ask which is the stronger of two ropes, an objective test can be made which will under similar conditions always give the same result, which renders it perfectly intelligible beforehand what is meant by stronger and which will be stronger. But between two motives the analogy fails utterly. First of all, it is psychologically false simplicity to speak of any such thing as a single motive; motives are always aspects of mental systems, and owe their strength to the system. Secondly, there is no objective criterion applicable to the measurement of motives, and thirdly, it follows that to call one stronger than the other must be a figure of speech, for at last the only way to define what we mean by the stronger motive is to say it is that which prevails, a completely circular process of demonstration. In the very cases where freedom seems most in evidence, that is, those in which the ordinary lines of choice are not applicable, determinism fails most utterly to predict what will happen. After the result, it tells us that the strongest motive prevailed, a useless piece of information. If the martyr Perpetua had yielded to the entreaty of her father and the dumb plea of her baby, which he held out to her, the determinist would tell us

The Idea of Man

that this was the strongest motive. Certainly it was the one which would be expected to prevail every time. But Perpetua chose her faith, so the undeterred determinist tells us that was the strongest motive. It is somewhat difficult to see by what means determinism of this type comes to think itself scientific, for anything more unlike the inductive methods of science could scarcely be imagined. One must admit the attractions of determinism in theory, and its advantages in the physical realm, but in practice, in the realm of minds, determinism cuts a sorry figure, and determinists are wise in confining themselves to threatening that they could demonstrate their theories in practice if only they had more data.

Determinism does not only fail in its prophecies, and the mark of the exactitude of science is its ability to prophesy, but it fails also in explanation of actual facts in mental life. It offers no alternative explanation of the intense sense of freedom all of us possess; of the will itself which is on deterministic lines a superfluity or an illusion; and of such facts as remorse, which as Illingworth said is 'only a darker name for man's conviction of his own freewill'. It is no reply to say that libertarians cannot explain these things, for the libertarian accepts them as facts, just as he accepts the psychological fact that we can retain and associate impressions. No one can explain why we are able to do so, but it is not needful, if we accept the fact. Determinism denies the facts freedom accepts, and therefore must at least try to explain why they appear to be what they are said not to be.

It often has been pleaded that determinism actually makes no change in our moral life. If we cannot help sinning, we cannot help punishing sin, and so no actual difference need take place. But this is incorrect for two reasons. As Streeter has said, the determinist admits that he cannot help arguing for determinism, and his opponent for freedom. The libertarian, on the other hand, contends that each is free to decide which is right. Therefore he only can logically dispute the matter, for if he is right in his view, his opinion is freely formed upon the issue, and he could presumably be converted to the opposite view. The determinist, if he is right, must admit that his views are not freely formed, that he sets them forth not because they convince him but because he cannot help it, and that he cannot be converted to the opposite view. Under such circumstances it is odd that he wishes to waste time in discussion.

Secondly, determinism takes all the reality out of life, making existence a puppet show. As well praise the day for being fine as the man for being heroic. One rebels against the robot universe determinism pictures, and when we ask what is the gain, we find that all is sacrificed to maintain the hypothesis, quite useless in practice, and based on a most doubtful analogy, that thought is determined as are the physical forces of the universe. The positive case for the existence of free will receives a contribution from the practice of the most rigid determinist who acts and speaks as if he were a free agent, and shows himself as sensitive to praise and blame as any one else. Such an attitude does not add to our trust in our own consciousness, for if it is so misleading that we are forced to act as if we were free when we are not, there is not much ground left upon which to defend the trustworthiness of consciousness against scepticism. If we are so misled by it in its testimony to its own nature, why trust it in its testimony as to the physical world? 'Who knoweth the things of a man, save the spirit of the man that is in him?' If consciousness, the spirit of the man, cannot tell us the truth about its own determination, but supplies us with a misleading sense of freedom, who shall say that it can be trusted in matters less particularly its own? Common sense denies determinism as it denies solipsism. It is sometimes said in reply that common sense believes in an external world which is in itself as it is to our senses, and that both realist and idealist agree that this is untenable. But the parallel fails when it is realized that both types of philosophy admit that consciousness is true in its testimony that something exists other than itself, whereas according to determinism, nothing exists corresponding to freedom. It is a sheer and inexplicable delusion.

There is, moreover, a curious paradox about deterministic argument in that the very idea of determinism is the invention of consciousness for the purpose of explaining the regularity of the physical universe. What has been postulated for a purpose is said by determinists to show that we cannot purpose, and our consciousness, like Frankenstein, is devoured by its own monster. Very few determinists have as much as acknowledged the part played by consciousness in creating the theory that is

The Idea of Man

subsequently used against the central feature of conscious existence, namely, purposiveness.

If, then, we may assume that nothing determinism advances can invalidate our sense of freedom, it remains to ask what this sense implies. Freedom is an ideal to which we approximate each in his degree rather than a state that is the same for all. In the physical world of the senses, everything seems to be determined strictly. With the appearance of life comes a state that chemico-physical laws do not fully explain, and with the higher animals there is a marked degree of spontaneity, and sometimes a surprising power of reversing the ordinary instinctive reactions under special circumstances. With man comes freedom, varying according to moral, even more than intellectual, powers. The lower types of mankind show comparatively few actions that are properly to be regarded as free, just as is the case with young children. Freedom comes with the development of the spiritual self, and its control over the animal self. Yet even so, only God can be said to be free, and herein lies the paradox of freedom that for God's freedom there are no alternatives, but His choice moves in one direction only, being directed to the best, so that the completest freedom is the same as the strictest necessity, save only that God is determined by Himself, and His is the only true self-determination. It is such considerations that lead us to conclude that determinism and freedom represent two aspects of life, neither of which is in itself final, for when taken up into the life of God they are one and the same thing. However strongly we may hold that whilst determinism is a characteristic of the physical universe as we see it, freedom is a characteristic of life as experienced.

It is along these lines that the old controversy of free will and necessity is likely to settle itself. On the lines of argument a stalemate sooner or later develops, as neither side will accept the same statement of the problem as the other. But as Bergson has shown, the crux of the problem is intellectual rather than factual. If we go to life itself, we find ourselves free, for freedom is a characteristic of actual reality. The real is living, free, self-developing. As soon as we try, however, mentally to recount the past and anticipate the future, we leave the timeless free present for the time-sequence, and in that sequence everything appears related to its predecessors, and hence the conclusion that it is determined. Freedom, as Kant said, is by reason of its very nature inexplicable. If it were explicable it would have to be determined. Hence we may, with Bergson, take freedom as a first-hand character of actually experienced reality, but grant the determinist that his position is the natural result of trying to place the timeless present in the time-sequence, and that in so far as we do this, we are led to think as if it were determined therein.

Chapter VI

The Idea of the Good

THE SCOPE OF ETHICS

THE philosophical approach to religion can hardly include a complete discussion of the problem of morality, and yet it cannot exclude altogether from its scope some consideration of the questions that are set before ethics. The term ethics is used in more than one sense. It may mean merely moral customs, as when we speak of the ethics of business or sport. It may mean teaching about morality, as when we speak of the ethics of Muhammad or Plato. It may also mean the scientific study of human conduct with reference to such predicates as right and good, which must include some attempt to say what we mean by the right and by the good. If we ask which of these, custom, teaching, theory, the term should signify, it appears that the first refers to morality rather than to ethics, and the second to teaching about morality rather than to the theory of morals, and if ethics denotes, as it should denote, scientific study, its proper connotation is the third of the three uses. Yet this cannot wholly exclude the other two. A rough analogy is afforded by the use of such a term as engineer. It may refer to the man who works an engine, or to the man who designs one, or to the professor of the science of engineering, which virtually are equivalent to the three uses above. The driver of an engine will be found to have a first-class working knowledge of his machine, and may be interested in some theoretical points, but his actual duties do not call for more than a practical acquaintance with engineering questions. The designer designs with a view to practical results. He may lack some of the knowledge of actual working conditions that the man on the footplate acquires. He may not know all the theoretical applications that the professor of engineering knows. His work brings him to a position between the other two. The professor may know little of actual working conditions, and may not have much experience of practical designing, though he is likely to be interested in both. His duty, however, is to deal with general principles apart from their embodiment in any particular engine.

The parallel with ethics is not distant. The ordinary man is concerned with practical morality, the teacher of morality with the application of moral rules to life, the student of ethics with the theory of morals, and though he is likely to have a keen interest in actual moral conditions and teaching, the science of ethics is not called on to provide a new morality for practice. Its province is to ask why conduct is called right or wrong, good or bad, and why it actually can be said to be so; what are the principles and aims of morals; what is the nature of the good and its relation to the right. Independent research on these questions marks out the scope of ethics as a science. The materials for ethics come from psychology and sociology, but these are descriptive studies, which are strictly limited to dealing with the actualities of experience as they are. Ethics is a normative science, dealing with what should be rather than with what is, even though it must consider the ideal with reference to the actual. But unlike logic and hygiene, which are normative sciences that lay down rules, ethics does not attempt to lay down any definite rule for conduct, since that would imply a generally accepted ideal. Ethics and aesthetics do not find any such accepted basis, and consequently are not able to lay down definite rules. The relation of ethics and art is bound to be close, for in a certain sense the good must be beautiful and the beautiful good, as the Greeks recognized by their compound word the 'beautiful-good'. Yet, as was said in an earlier chapter, aesthetics does not deal necessarily with what is morally beautiful, whilst ethics does not deal with what is beautiful but not moral, so that despite philosophers like Herbart, who made ethics a part of aesthetics, the spheres of the two are tolerably clearly distinguished. Art and morality are independent interests, however closely they become related in the unity of human life.

The connexion between ethics and metaphysics will depend rather on our conception of metaphysics than of ethics. If metaphysics is limited to the consideration of what is logically self-consistent, then it must be kept apart from ethical considerations by reason of the fact that logic knows no bridge from what is to what should be, and that is why the Hegelian

The Idea of the Good

writers who promised a basis for ethics in metaphysics never provided any such thing. There is more promise in the hint which, in the closing paragraph of his *Metaphysics*, Lotze threw out in saying that 'the true beginning of metaphysics lies in ethics'. The living meaning of the world is the foundation of its facts. If there is any purpose in the universe, such purpose may explain its creation and constitution, and the end to which we should strive, and in that case the suggestion that the good might be the basis of the true would find fulfilment. Yet at any such purpose we can but guess, and to guess is no foundation for any science. Apart from such a unifying purpose, ethics and metaphysics seem bound to remain separately pursuing their ends, not because there is any opposition between them, nor any need for separation, but simply because we cannot put together in any one consistent whole our convictions as to the relation of the good to the true, or link that which we believe to be, with that which we not less strongly believe ought to be. The realms of fact and of value use coinage so utterly different that it seems impossible to exchange from one currency to the other. Yet that need not be taken as a denial of the possibility of such exchange, could we find how to make it.

THEORIES OF THE GOOD

Pleasure as the Good

THAT the end man should seek was pleasure, in the sense, at any rate, of that which afforded him happiness, was admitted by most of the early schools of Greek thought. Even Aristotle, who remarked that, judged by the lives they led, most men, including the lowest types, identified happiness with pleasure, conceded there was some ground for their doing so. It seemed that, as a matter of fact, men did and always would seek happiness, and what was advisable was not to discuss whether this should be so, but to accept the fact, and show what was the true road to happiness. From the beginning, therefore, psychological hedonism, the doctrine that pleasure is the root motive of action, lay at the basis of the ethical type of hedonism that declared it should be so. Yet as Sidgwick, at any rate, saw, the two are at heart inconsistent, for if every one does seek simply his own pleasure, to tell us that we are to seek that of others can avail only if we can be persuaded that thereby we shall increase our own, a doctrine that may be prudential, yet hardly moral.

Christian influences checked the growth of pleasure philosophies for many centuries. The first sign of their revival came with Hobbes, who was persuaded that the pleasures of power were the sole motive. Hobbes exercised more influence on his critics than on his friends. Few followed his ideas, but right down to the time of Butler, with his admissions as to the necessity of 'reasonable self-love', it is plain that Hobbes's views had impressed themselves even upon those who set out to challenge them, and it is not surprising that in the eighteenth century we find such writers as Tucker and Paley developing a utilitarian ethics which was to find its fuller embodiment in Bentham, Mill, and Sidgwick. Mill, with more candour than logic, frankly declared that the only proof possible or needful that the general happiness was desirable, was that each desired his own, a remark that witnesses to the fact that the strength of utilitarian ethics is derived from the notion that pleasure must necessarily guide our actions.

It is, more than anything else, the psychological falsity of that notion which has contributed to the decline of hedonism. Not only must the impulse to act precede the pleasure that may be gained by acting, hunger, for example, must precede the pleasure of eating, but unconscious motivation affords a definite example of actions that cannot in any intelligible sense be said to be done to avoid pain or pursue pleasure. One might as well argue that the migrating swallow goes abroad for the pleasure of spending the winter in Africa, as argue that the actions that proceed from some instinctive 'drive', whether conscious or unconscious, are done for the sake of pleasure. The opponents of hedonism often urged the paradox to which hedonism was exposed in that most pleasures depend on something else, and deliberately to seek them is usually to diminish them. Many a pleasure-seeker after a night of gaiety finds himself in the position of those who have toiled all night and caught nothing. Some pleasures, are not much diminished by being sought, but it still obtains that pleasure is an exception to the rule that he that seeketh findeth. The confusion which lies at the root of Hedonism is between the gratification that comes whenever

The Idea of the Good

what has been deliberately willed, is attained, and pleasure in an unqualified sense. If a dead-tired man who loathes the taste of stimulants takes brandy to whip his jaded body to complete some hard task, can he be said to take it for pleasure as the epicure drinks some old vintage at a dinner? To say that he acts thus for the pleasure of completing his task cannot be true if the task is some unwelcome duty. If then, the reply is that the act is done for the pleasure of doing the duty, it is simply to play with words. There may be a certain grim sense of satisfaction that the unwelcome task is over, but to call that the agreeable feeling, pleasure, such as the epicure desires, is fantastic. The psychological assumptions of hedonism are false, and the last and greatest exponent of the doctrine, Sidgwick, was wise in denying that psychological hedonism afforded a basis for ethical hedonism.

The palmy days of the pleasure-philosophy lasted for more than a century from the enunciation of the doctrine by Bentham till the death of Sidgwick in 1900. Bentham coined the phrase 'greatest happiness principle', and adopted from Priestley the celebrated maxim 'the greatest happiness of the greatest number', although finally he abandoned the notion, owing to some realization of the impossibility of equating quantity and quality of pleasures. Mill, adapting Bentham's use of the term utility to denote the tendency to produce happiness, gave the name utilitarianism, and both he and Sidgwick found the hardest part of their exposition that which sought to prove that the pleasures of others should weigh equally with our own. It is one thing to show that the wider the field in which happiness is sought the more likely is the happiness gained to be satisfactory, and another to prove that this field includes the happiness of all sentient beings.

Perhaps the best form of hedonism is that which regards pleasure as a calculus, or ground of preference in the choice between alternative possibilities. Just as the thermometer is the test of heat, so may it be said that pleasure is the test of action. If in the widest and wisest sense this course of action will produce more pleasure than that, it is therefore to be preferred.

This, however, involves more than pleasure simply. To ask whether the purchase of a book will give more pleasure than the purchase of a cigar can hardly be answered without some comparison between the values of reading and smoking. But as soon as we admit that one is better intellectually, the other physically, we have left pleasure pure and simple as a criterion. Pleasure is 'adjectival'. There is no such thing as pleasure taken by itself. Always must it be that pleasure is found in connexion with some object, pursuit, and so forth, and that in which the pleasure lies makes all the difference to the character of the pleasure. Hedonism cannot admit that, however, without denying its own basis. Its fatal weakness lay in treating pleasure apart from that which affords pleasure.

Still further, hedonism disregarded the self that was pleased. It is not simply a matter of satisfying our wants, that is set before us, but of satisfying ourselves, and what pleases one side of the self may by no means please another side. Hedonism never realized that a man may be happy in suffering and unhappy in his pleasure seeking. Pleasure then, taken simply as such, fails to afford any criterion to guide our actions, and therefore fails as an ethical end. That hedonism enjoyed so lengthy a vogue may be traced to the fact that happiness is a universal quest, but what hedonism overlooked in stressing that perfectly correct statement was that happiness loses its meaning when taken apart from reference to the kind of happiness it represents, and the side of the self that is made happy. Hedonism confused pleasure with happiness, despite the fact that Aristotle clearly saw the difference between the two. Yet even if we substitute the term happiness for pleasure, it still remains that happiness, as such, in the unqualified sense given to the notion by utilitarians, cannot be made to serve in any practical sense as a guide to activity.

One last point may be mentioned which the classical hedonists, as we might call them, failed entirely to recognize. Whatever we take as the ultimate good, it must surely be a good that is capable of developing to higher stages with its pursuit. Pleasure is essentially static. It may be said that we can rise from lower to higher types of pleasure, but the point at once arises in what sense can pleasures be said to be higher and lower, and it is evident that it is not as pleasures that they can be so, but as possessing some other worth, and, when that is admitted, we are clearly departing from the notion that pleasure is the only good. Those who reject hedonism do not reject the

The Idea of the Good

place and value of pleasure in life, or deny that some pleasures are to be sought rather than others. What they do deny is the central doctrine of all hedonism that pleasure is the essential end in life.

Perfection as the Good

That the ethical end is perfection has often been set forth, but so varied have been the ideas of what is meant by perfection, that one cannot speak of perfectionism as a definite school of thought. Rather is it a general name for many heterogeneous tendencies. In some respects it is the same as Aristotle's 'eudaimonism'. The name has also been applied to the 'evolutionary' ethics of the period immediately following Darwin. Or again, those who have advocated self-realization as the ethical end have shared in the name. In some hands the notion of self-realization has not been presented as a moral end, for example Nietzsche's superman, whose perfection seems to most minds the reverse of what is to be understood by morality. Its best embodiment is found in the thought of T. H. Green, who fought a gallant fight against the prevailing unspiritual ethics of his day. Green maintained that man was essentially spiritual, and that the moral end must therefore be expressed in spiritual terms. Under Hegel's influence, Green interpreted the spiritual as the rational, declaring that we must live according to the rational self, which was the self of deepest insight and wisdom. This, he held, would fulfil Kant's demand for self-consistency as the essence of a moral act, and the claim of hedonism also, since the result of so living would be happiness. The expression rational self suffers, however, from much indefiniteness. In the narrower sense the rational is certainly not the same as the moral. A man, unable to swim, who jumps into the water to attempt to save someone from drowning is not acting rationally, but none the less, his act excites our moral admiration. If, on the other hand, we make the term rational wide enough to include such acts, it loses its meaning, and conveys little information as to the character of what is to be thought ideal. Green admitted that the ideal must be to some extent unknown, and it is exactly because no one can define perfection that perfectionism has little meaning as a moral theory.

The Philosophical Approach to Religion

Evolutionary Ethics

The idea that man's moral duty is to follow Nature is at least as old as Lao-Tse and indeed certainly older. Heaven, he declared, does not strive or advertise its ways. The flowers grow, fulfil their cycle of life, and fade. If man but copied the works of Nature, living according to inward impulse, not outward ends, he would likewise fulfil his destiny, untroubled and untroubling. Lao's ethics inculcated inactivity. Man must live unmoved by life and death. Silence is the best speech, and stillness the heart of wisdom. The more practical system of Confucius appealed to the mind of China more than Lao's philosophic quietism, but the notion of following Nature never wholly lacked adherents right down to the days of Rousseau. In the whirlpool of thought that followed Darwin's ideas the notion of putting ethics upon a 'scientific' basis obsessed not a few thinkers. Spencer dreamed of such adjustment of the individual to his environment that, by simply following his own impulses, man will act so as to secure the complete happiness of himself and others. What he failed to see was that morality is not a matter of natural selection, but a human struggle against it. Moreover, Spencer finds no place for moral effort, despite what he said about man assisting in the process of adaptation. Adaptation may be, sometimes indeed is, by relaxation and even degeneration, rather than effort. We drift into adaptation with environment. The whole history of moral progress is written in terms of those who have reached beyond their present environment to some ideal not yet existent. Then again, there is no reason to declare that the survival of the species is the ethical good. As William Booth once told a man who pleaded in extenuation of his malpractices that he 'had to live', there is no necessity why any man should live, but much why he should do right. The survival of the fittest is far from being the same thing as moral progress. If the 'fittest' survive, it means no more than if we said those who happened to be best placed got the best view, or that those in the rear coaches survived in a head-on collision, whereas in a rear collision those in the front coaches would survive. The fittest are those who happen to survive under the particular conditions. There is no moral aspect in such survival.

The Idea of the Good

The position of the social welfare school fails similarly to afford any satisfactory theory of morals. To say that we should seek the perfect equilibrium of society, and that morality consists in that which makes thereto, presumes that such an end is a good in itself. One need not agree. A society of cannibals may be excellently equilibrated within itself, as were no doubt the celebrated Assassins. It is true that every form of society tends to maintain its actual equilibrium, and to resent the reformer who tries to upset it, but that does not make it evident that the reformer may not be leading to a better type of society. The notion, however, has been adopted by most writers of this school, that what tends in the long run to survive is that which makes for such social equilibrium. Yet even so, what evidence have we that such a state of things should be? What we are told is that this type of conduct does survive. What we need to ask is whether it should, and why. The attempt to construct an evolutionary ethics, whatever be its source, always meets this difficulty that a process of evolution shows us what does happen, but morality is concerned with what should happen. The *reductio ad absurdum* of evolutionary ethics was supplied by Nietzsche's idea of the new race of supermen. In one sense Nietzsche was consistent. He did not accept the equilibrium of society as it is, but looked to a new and better type of society, better at least from his point of view. But there is no reason why the matter should stop here. A race of super-supermen would be the next step, and so on, until at last the fate of the supermen would be that of the famous Kilkenny cats! It may be true that we who are constituted socially by our nature have an inner tendency therein to act according to that which leads towards social equilibrium, in the main at least. If, so that is a sociological fact rather than an ethical law, and the real weakness of this type of thinking is that it offers sociology for ethics. Mere equilibrium is the law of inaction rather than progress, and unless we accept the dangerous mistake that evolution and progress mean the same thing, evolutionary doctrine forms by itself no basis for ethics.

Ethical Intuitionism

The difficulty of defining the moral end has lent force to the attitude of those who claim that it can be known only by intuition. The older type of intuitionism or intuitionalism such as Martineau represented cannot be maintained. Martineau held that the centre of the moral judgement was in the fact that we perceived intuitively a difference of worth between any two conflicting impulses, and he drew up a table of 'springs of action' according to their moral worth. That is based upon a psychological position that has definitely passed away. But a revival of a modified intuitionism is found in Dr. Moore's assertion that 'good' is a simple and unanalysable conception, however much we may differ as to 'the good'. Although there has been comparatively little support for the position, there has been also a lack of decisiveness in the criticisms passed upon it, which indicates that those who are not prepared to agree, are not able to refute the contention of Dr. Moore by showing exactly what is conveyed by the conception of good. Most of the criticism centres round the idea that good is an exceedingly ambiguous term, and that Dr. Moore's usage of the term simplifies it unduly by trying to make the notion of good independent of the actual choice between alternatives regarded as good and bad. It is also urged that good may mean both that which has some value for any end, and that which is morally good, and in the latter sense it is not incapable of definition.

Yet it seems to be going altogether too far to suggest that when we pass moral judgements upon conduct we are always conscious of the standard from which we pass them, and when we say anything is morally good, we mean it is that which should be chosen as promoting happiness, social integration, perfection or whatever else it is. Only professional moralists, acting in their professional capacity, are likely to do any such thing. Whether or not 'good' is unanalysable, it seems certain that the ordinary man does not try to analyse what he means by it. Intuitionist theories of morals bear witness, however, to a fact that is highly significant. To draw up lists of intuitively known moral truths, as did some of the Cambridge Platonists; to treat conscience as a kind of common abstract human faculty as did Butler; or perhaps more especially as did his imitators; to make a table of 'springs of action' of self evident moral precedence, as did Martineau, are all methods which genetic psychology has rendered obsolete. What remains, however, is the fact that the tendency to show approval, and more markedly

The Idea of the Good

disapproval, of the actions of others, belongs to the inborn intuitive law of the pack. True, the pack is more prone to punish than to reward, its approval being silent where its disapproval is shown by tooth and claw, but man, as a social being must have shared this tendency, and as he developed mentally would show signs of definite approval as well as of anger. At a still higher stage, he must have learned to judge his own actions as well as those of others, and finally created standards in tribal law by which he professed to judge.

Westermarck is not far from fact, therefore, in his contention that there is an emotional root behind moral judgements, but it does not seem to follow that he is right in assuming that they are therefore merely subjective. We do not postulate a moral 'instinct'. Too many instincts have already been postulated, and little is done in any case by postulating them. But we must assume that moral judgements have a root in this sense in inborn propensities, and that is why, like instinctive activities generally, they are apt to be regular in the main, but irregular in the exception, to make towards the preservation of the species and individual as a whole, whilst sometimes showing aberrancies fatal to the individual. Yet it seems impossible to assume that anything so universal and so important as the moral life of mankind can be rooted in anything else than human nature itself, and to argue that morality arises from an effort to seek some end such as pleasure, perfection, or whatever else, is to look at one aspect of the process, that which is furthest away from its origins. It would seem, therefore, that moralists have been too definite in asking what is the ethical end to which conduct is to be directed, and not less so in assuming, as most of them have done, one definite end before all. If we are right in assuming that the roots of the moral sense lie in that dim instinctive activity that is manifested in the law of animal social organization, it appears that it is directed from its origins rather than from its end. Man is made so that he cannot be indifferent to all types of action, but finds himself affected by sentiments of approval and disapproval. By long years of experience, humanity has organized these sentiments, and attached them to the various codes, traditions, laws of the race, but the tendency to be affected by the good and the bad is as much inborn as the tendency to be affected by the ugly and the beautiful. The tiny child who cries 'Pretty' or 'Nasty' is not supposed to be judging from any definite standard of art, and man's moral judgements are at root of the same kind. But the greater importance of conduct to life has made them more urgent, so that a theory of right and wrong is a much more vital matter than a theory of beauty and ugliness.

It may seem that this implies that man is possessed with some half-blind semi-instinctive sense of the values of conduct in its bearing upon the life and preservation of the group, much the same as the pack law of the herd, and that under the chance guidance of experience this has become more or less organized into the moral law, and attributed to various sources, the will of the god, the law of things as they are, the tendency to seek pleasure, or to strive to perfection, and so forth. It may be asked what is the difference between this view and that named above, that morality is a matter of social welfare. The answer is that we must distinguish, as the evolutionary moralists failed to do, the ideal from the actual. We may agree with the evolutionary theory of morals that there is a tendency in man that makes for social well-being. It is hardly possible to imagine the evolution of social life, whether in man or animal otherwise, but in itself this is not enough.

The Basis of Moral Authority

Any such tendency lacks the character of an 'ought' which is what is distinctive in morality. As Green said (*Prolegomena*, p. 11): 'It is obvious that to a being who is simply the result of natural forces an injunction to conform to their laws is unmeaning.' That we may possess a tendency to act in a certain way is one thing, but it is another to say that we ought so to act. Despite the vehemence of those who say that morality needs no 'supernatural sanctions' that right is its own authority, and he who does not see this cannot be made to recognize any other authority, it remains that it is religion, in the widest sense of that word, which actually gives authority to our moral sense. That is to say, the authority of the moral law turns ultimately upon our interpretation of the universe, and a spiritual interpretation gives an authority to the moral sense that a naturalistic interpretation cannot give.

The Idea of the Good

The reason is as follows. Moral law is either subjective or objective. If subjective, it has no more authority than our preferences, or shall we say, than conventionally accepted rules of etiquette. If it is objective, then it exists as the ultimate laws of the universe exist, discovered, but not invented, by our minds. They are supposed to be laws of what is, or as realists think, of what nature is apart from us. But the moral law is not a law of what nature is, nor of what man is, but of what should be, and therefore must belong to mind which alone can conceive it and express it. If the moral law is objective it must be the expression of the spiritual reality of the universe, as the laws of Nature are held to be the expression of its physical character. That is to say, it depends upon a spiritual conception of reality, which to all intents means that it must be regarded as the law of God.

There are non-theistic systems of morals, but they usually claim for their teaching a greater authority than it can intrinsically possess. Though moral systems historically have almost always drawn their ultimate authority from religion, they are seldom in need of appealing to that authority, since, being acknowledged, they are accepted without question. This fact has served the non-theistic systems well.

It may be admitted that there can be a morality apart from any reference to God. The teaching of orthodox Buddhism is a case in point, but none the less, even here, morals are based on a metaphysic that affords a conception of the ultimate nature of the universe as it is held to be. Any moral law that is not so based cannot be called objective. Can we abandon the idea that the moral law is objective? It is the most definite conviction we possess that to do right is better than to do wrong. We have learned to revise our conceptions of what were taught to us as fundamental laws of Nature. We read that a distinguished scientist has openly questioned whether all the so-called laws of Nature may not be laws of our minds, and the quantum laws the only real example of a law of Nature itself. But nothing would persuade us that it can ever be better to be selfish than unselfish, cruel than kind, to hate men than to love them. In that sense, the moral law is more absolute than any law of Nature. If it is subjective merely, just the expression of sentiments that happen to have evolved in us,

The Philosophical Approach to Religion

what law can be called objective? Surely if anything belongs to the nature of things as they are, it must be the fundamental principles of moral life. The authority of the moral law may be explained away, but it cannot be explained on any purely humanistic hypothesis. The moral law as actual may be traced back to its sources in the nature of man. But its authority does not lie in itself as actual, but in its ideal, and that cannot be found behind, but only ahead. Apart, therefore, from regarding the moral law as simply the consolidated voice of the race, which can allow it only a prudential, not an absolute authority, there is only one alternative, that of regarding it as objective, and based upon the actual nature of reality. But not of physical reality. There is no ground of morals in what is, only in the spiritual conception of what should be. Morality must find its ultimate basis in values, and in those values that belong to the very nature of reality, which is, for theism at least, the same as saying the very nature of God.

Chapter VII

God and the World

THE POLYTHEISTIC STAGE

THE denunciations of the Hebrew prophets against idolatry and polytheism have placed the polytheistic conception of the relation of heaven and earth in a light perhaps unduly unfavourable. It is likely that polydaemonism, belief in a multiplicity of spirits, some worshipped and some ignored, preceded polytheism, and represented the legacy of animistic ideas. Polytheism proper developed as the gods were more definitely recognized with names and functions.

The causes that led to the development of polytheism are conjectural. Jevons (*Introduction to the History of Religion*, ch. xviii) offers several suggestions, though most anthropologists are not inclined to agree that the fusion of totems played a great part therein. But where there was a fusion of tribes or clans, the various cults of gods and ancestors would also more or less combine, especially through intermarriage. Even such a monarch as Solomon had to make provision for the gods of his wives. Where the gods had no distinctive name or characteristic, it would not be difficult to amalgamate them with others, but on the other hand, if some functional god's function grew in importance, automatically that fact would exalt him to a place of power. Sometimes the god who had been the supreme god of some clan or tribe, became a departmental deity, with some specific function in the larger nation into which the tribe became merged. The Baalim were fertility gods, and as Jahveh was a 'God of the hills', it seemed reasonable to Hebrew agriculturists, despite the prophets, to keep in right relation to the local Baal. There are also cases where the worship of one god at two festivals rent the god in twain, and the two parts grew separately. Similarly amongst some peoples, especially the Semites, the goddesses are clearly in many cases invented as spouses for the gods, with functions that are but a reflection of theirs.

The Philosophical Approach to Religion

There can scarcely be a theoretical side of polytheism. It belongs to a stage of development when the gods were thought of as persons, not problems. Mythology supplied what might be called the theory of polytheism in that the myths set forth the relations of the gods to one another and to man. The existence of such myths made it difficult for polytheistic ideas to rise in step with moral development, and that is why Plato wished to expurgate the myths of Homer and others from his scheme of education. Because a monotheistic deity develops later, and less can be said of him than of gods who are in relation to other gods, mythology has not been the same barrier to monotheism as to polytheism. Yet apart from this, it is not easy to show why polytheism is necessarily offensive. It is less harmful to worship than deism, less to morality than pantheism. Objections to polytheism, as Deutero-Isaiah saw them, lie in the vanity of idolatry, or as St. Paul saw them, in the immoralities of polytheist nations. Yet neither idolatry nor immorality is necessarily attached to polytheism. Islam, which regards polytheism as the worst of sins, is able only to give this reason, that it robs the one God of His due in service and worship.

William James pointed out that a radical pluralism could not object to polytheism as a theory of the divine nature. Philosophic theism, he declared, tended to pantheism; popular religion was frankly pluralistic, not to say polytheistic (*Varieties of Religious Experience*, p. 131). Polytheism 'has always been the religion of common people and is so still to-day' (*Ibid.*, p. 526). The popular attitude towards the Trinity is much more reminiscent of three persons than one God. The saints fulfil the functions of many of the old polytheistic deities, and had the Church been unwilling to recognize patron saints, it would have had much more difficulty in dealing with popular forms of worship. There is no doubt James was justified, but such an outcry arose that later (*A Pluralistic Universe*, p. 310) he surrendered, and said that, as it gave offence, the term polytheism need not be used.

Polytheism, then, is not in itself irreligious. It represents a stage that was natural, and indeed inevitable, in the childhood of religion. That is the reason why it is no longer a serious conception of the relation of the divine to the human. It has

God and the World

failed to keep its place, and has been left behind, with the development of thought. The Christian Church convinced the civilized world of the superiority of the Hebrew conception of God, and the polytheistic conceptions of the Empire faded away before it. Greek philosophy had pointed in the same direction as Hebrew religion. For the educated, polytheism was discredited before Christianity came to destroy its appeal to the unlearned. Polytheism receded, left behind rather than actually confuted. It proved unfit to survive as a philosophical or as a religious conception of God. Unless some radical pluralist can set forth some convincing arguments why the divine nature should be regarded as a multiplicity of spirits rather than one spirit, polytheism seems destined to remain in the limbo of things superseded. That task has not been seriously attempted. Perhaps it cannot be. Until it is, we can leave polytheism where the tide of time has left it.

THE PANTHEISTIC CONCEPTION

PANTHEISM is the equation God = the existent, whether the existent is spiritually or materialistically conceived. The completest system of pantheism known to history is that of the Indian Vedanta. In Western philosophy it was represented in the Eleatic school, especially in Parmenides' development of the teaching of Xenophanes. The Stoics professed, as Lecky put it, 'an ill-defined uncertain and somewhat inconsistent pantheism'. From them the line of thought runs through the Gnostics and the Neoplatonists, reappears in the jumbled theories of the Kabbala, and shows itself in the writings of Erigena, Bruno, Spinoza and Schopenhauer, though none of these, not even Spinoza, is to be called consistently and uncompromisingly pantheistic. Absolute idealism has a ready inclination towards pantheism, as all monistic systems have had, when they have received any religious interpretation. Hegel has been accused of pantheism more than once. He has been defended by charging the critics with failure to understand what Hegel implied by the Absolute, yet in that failure at times Hegel himself seems to share! In addition to philosophical pantheisms, there have been such poetic pantheisms as those of Shelley and Emerson, whilst some years ago, a Mr. Allanson

Picton, who claimed to be a Spinozist, attempted not only a pantheistic philosophy but a pantheistic religion, which rejected the materialistic aspect of Spinoza's 'Substance' in favour of its spiritual aspect, and stressed the 'intellectual love of God'. But as Flint said long ago (*Anti-Theistic Theories*, p. 376), pantheism 'is always in unstable equilibrium between theism and atheism, and is logically necessitated to elevate itself into the one or to descend to the other'. The justice of the phrase 'unstable equilibrium' is shown by the fact that in most of the instances given above, especially in the case of Erigena, it would be possible to make a case to prove that the writer was a monist insisting on immanence of the divine in creation, and misrepresented as a pantheist.

In the main, there have been four avenues leading to pantheism. One has been through philosophy. The difference between any rigid monism and pantheism lies simply in attaching or not attaching religious predicates to the All. Theologically, it has been approached by strong insistence on immanence, omnipotence and omnipresence. It is this which has actually introduced pantheistic features into the development of the uncompromising monotheism of Islam, especially amongst the Sufis of the sixth century. A third approach is through poetry and art, for the all-comprehensive sweep of pantheism, which brings the manifold multiplicity of existence down to one root, one base, one meaning, appeals to the imagination, appeals indeed more to it than to reason. Finally, mysticism has never been far removed from pantheism, for reasons similar to those just stated. Most of the great mystics have been far more truly pantheists than theists, though their language of devotion has concealed the fact, not only from others but sometimes from themselves.

Monism may be consistent. Pantheism never is. It personalises the All, if it is to serve as a religion, for it is historically true, despite what Bradley once said about a personal God not being an essential to religion, that no race has ever continued to worship an impersonal principle. In ancient Greece, and in modern India, pantheism has been constantly unequally yoked with polytheism. In India, where pantheism is found in its most marked form, polytheism is more prevalent than in any other country. It cannot be that this is accidental. Pantheism,

God and the World

unable itself to satisfy the aspirations of the religious consciousness, is obliged to allow polytheism to supply what it cannot give, and to excuse itself by the consideration that polytheism expresses the pervading character of the divine in life in a way 'understanded of the people'.

Pantheism has never resolved the dilemma of a choice between God as the All in its concrete fulness, the bad and the good indifferently, or God as a principle so abstract that, like the One Beyond Intelligence of Plotinus, He is uncharacterizable. Neither conception has any of the values of the idea of God, and hence the justice of the gibe that pantheism is 'painted atheism'. Pantheism reduces morality and our moral sense to a superfluity. It cannot admit the distinctions that are implied therein. Many pantheists, like the Stoics, for example have been strict moralists, but this is another example of the inconsistency of the pantheistic creed. It has been replied that God is the All, and therefore no part taken by itself is God. A particular smear of paint is part, and a needful part, of an oil painting, but in itself it may be ugly and disproportionate. Seen in relation to the whole, it loses these characteristics and is transformed by the rest of the picture. So it is suggested may it be with evil and God. The answer is that the All is an unrealizable conception, and to call it God is possible only because we do not know what it represents. Yet there is as much or as little reason to call it the devil as God. If pure being is equivalent to pure nothing, it may also be said that everything, in the all inclusive sense given to that phrase by pantheism, is just as much nothing as everything. Like the Buddhist nirvana, it is the opposite of all that is characterizable, and for that reason it must be uncharacterizable. It is, therefore, as much to be called nothing as everything, just as the case with the concept of nirvana. The accommodating nature of pantheism is illustrated by the fact that the materialist Haeckel called it the world system of the modern scientist, in which God as an intra-mundane being, in contrast with the theistic idea of an extra-mundane God, was identical with nature and operative as energy. In which case one wonders, why confuse language by calling energy God? Yet at the same time Mr. Picton was insisting that a materialistic unity was unacceptable to science, and that pantheism supplied both science and religion with a spiritual unity, God.

The Philosophical Approach to Religion

In short, pantheism can be anything that is required of it. It talks about the All, but as no words can characterize the All, it selects any aspect of that All, that it prefers, and uses it as denoting its character, whilst telling us that no part, nothing less than the All, will serve. Perhaps the most consistent forms of pantheism have been those of Schopenhauer and Von Hartmann, where the All was regarded as unconscious will, and pantheism was linked with that pessimism which is the opposite of religion, instead of receiving a religious interpretation. There might be a similar pantheism to-day centred round the 'Life-Urge'. The root defect of pantheism is the inconsequence of its persistence in calling the All, God. It is as truly pan-atheism as pan-theism. If the All is one, that is no reason for worshipping it. The pantheist replies that we cannot help worshipping, and that the All is the worthiest object of worship. That is obviously to assume that worthiness is quantitative not qualitative, which is just the point that pantheism should prove and never attempts to prove. It is true, however, that historically the All neither originated worship nor has ever succeeded in maintaining itself as the object of genuine and continued worship. The attempt of pantheism to attach religious predicates to its monism may serve to conceal the abstract nakedness of all rigid monisms, may perhaps give some satisfaction to the craving for an object of worship, but is a proceeding as vain as that of the Roman empire which strove to make good the barrenness of its decaying religious faith by deifying Caesar.

Pantheism has been a theory seldom radically carried out. Such essays as Tennyson's 'Higher Pantheism' are simply assertions of immanence, and must be regarded as panentheistic rather than pantheistic, in the strict sense. Monism has always had the reputation both in theology and philosophy of being, one almost said, more 'respectable' than pluralism. Yet every monist who brings religion into his monism finds himself on the slope that falls uninterruptedly towards pantheism. Few have dared to go all the way down. Sooner or later they have retraced their steps, compromising their monism in doing so, yet witnessing to the fact that in the end the abstract has always to bow the knee to the concrete, and that life, not logic, has the last word.

God and the World

THE DEISTIC CONCEPTION

THE distinction between deism and theism is now generally recognized, but it is one that grew gradually, and the chief characteristics of the historical deists are scarcely denoted by the modern notion that deism is the theory of a transcendent God who set the world process going and left it to its own devices. Samuel Clarke distinguished four classes of opinion on this matter. First, men who believed in a God utterly unconcerned with this world's government. Next, those who held that there was no future life, since God was wholly transcendent and did not administer rewards or punishments, which to the eighteenth century was the chief reason for a future life. But he included neither as deist. Nor did he call deists those who believed in a providence that worked of necessity in the ordering of the world, but was not moral governance. 'The only true deists' were those who believed in moral government, but not revelation, from which they would expunge all inconsistent with 'natural religion', whilst still calling themselves Christians. This affiliates the deists with natural religion, and supports the contention of Leland that Lord Herbert of Cherbury was the progenitor of deism. The actual term deism came into use about the beginning of the eighteenth century, and the phrase 'God but not the Gospel' was used by opponents to characterize the nature of deistic beliefs. Judged by the writings of the deists themselves, it is evident that the actual characteristics of historical deism were of this type, and not those now associated with the term.

The deistic position had a powerful supporter in Locke, whose idea of God was of the deistic type, and whose treatment of Christianity was in effect rationalistic. Locke, however, disliked the deists, and was annoyed if any claimed him as one of them. Deism was in bad odour amongst the orthodox, as savouring of 'freethinking', and Locke, with influential friends, a man well thought of by the government, was in no wise inclined to be reckoned amongst the disparagers of Christianity. Moreover, Locke held the necessity of revelation, at any rate for the unlearned who were not guided in conduct by reason. Locke died just as the deist movement was beginning to assume its most influential phase, but there is little doubt that his apologetic,

The Philosophical Approach to Religion

the *Reasonableness of Christianity*, so severely simplified the essentials of Christian faith, that those who wished to ignore revelation altogether, found in it a line of attack rather than of defence.

The actual deist movement was short-lived, lasting from the end of the seventeenth to the end of the eighteenth century. It was almost entirely British, though Leland speaks of 'deists' in France and Italy a hundred years before the British movement began. Its influence failed to spread through other European countries, notwithstanding that Voltaire and Rousseau show traces of deistic ideas in more than one respect.

Toland, in 1696, led the way to the central phase of deism in his book *Christianity not Mysterious*, which had the distinction of being ordered to be burnt by the Irish Parliament, an advertisement of which Toland was not slow to take advantage. He declared that there was no reason to assert that there was in God or His attributes anything that transcended the ability of reason to comprehend. Indeed the incomprehensible was the false. He boldly claimed that the original meaning of 'mystery' was simply a 'secret' that could be imparted to the initiated, and that the connotation 'unfathomable' was due to alien and heathen ideas that had corrupted the simplicity of the Gospel. Collins followed up what Toland had begun in a book which bears an interesting title, *Discourse of Freethinking occasioned by the Rise and Growth of a Sect Called Freethinkers*, in which he contended for the unalienable right of every individual to judge for himself in religious matters. He argued that free thought had in every way made for progress, and found plenty of examples of destructive and reactionary results where it had been restrained. It did not occur to Collins any more than to the modern 'freethinkers' that any thought that does not coincide with theirs can possibly be 'free'.

Collins turned subsequently to the role of attack, aiming his blows against miracles and prophecy, the two main redoubts defended by Butler and the apologists, and tried to impugn not only on the accuracy, but on the good faith of the evangelists. It was left to Tindal, a fellow of All Souls, Oxford, to restore the controversy to better lines by the publication in 1730 of *Christianity as Old as Creation*, in which he sought to prove that the constancy of God made it certain that there

God and the World

could be no fundamental difference between natural religion and any revelation given from Him. Whatever in Christianity was of God must therefore be in harmony with natural religion. Tindal did not think of the possibility of reversing this statement. Like the other deists, he accepted natural religion as the norm, and reason, as the deists understood it, as the final arbiter.

The end of deism came suddenly. The last phase of the conflict centred round the attack on miracles and prophecy, and generated a heat that the more academic discussion upon natural theology and revelation could not produce. Deist writers alienated sympathy from themselves by falling into vituperative language, which ill accorded with the decorous temper of the age that frowned upon all excess and 'enthusiasm' whether for or against religious beliefs. Moreover, the mass of the people were in no mood to join in a wholesale attack on Christianity. Though Butler could lament in 1736 that it had come to be taken for granted by many that 'Christianity is not so much as a subject of inquiry, but that it is now at length discovered to be fictitious,' there was no great inclination outside deist circles to reject openly the religion that was, to the mind of the age, so closely associated with respectability and the upholding of the needful moral and social sanctions. The *Analogy* came as a powerful antidote to the reasonings of Tindal. Gradually the issue began to lose importance. The rise of Methodism was not unconnected with this decline. Wesley brought a new centre of religious interest, and also of controversy. It became a matter of meeting this fresh menace of 'enthusiasm', and the controversialists turned from the deists to the new foe.

Wesley himself answered deism by his works rather than his words. He made God a reality. He brought men face to face with the mystery of redeeming love. In a letter to Lord Rawdon, written in 1760, he confesses, 'I have been afraid lest you should exchange the Simplicity of the Gospels for a Philosophical Religion. O my Lord, why should we go one step farther than this, We love Him, because He first loved us?' About the same time an unexpected blow fell upon the deist cause. Hume, in his *Natural History of Religion*, exploded the idea of religion as old as creation, of the few simply sufficient truths concerning re-

The Philosophical Approach to Religion

ligion and morals that deists presumed were the natural heritage of all men. Hume showed that this picture was grotesquely unlike the actual religious beliefs of early peoples, and with this death blow to its academic ideas, deism faltered and fell. In some part, its heritage went to philosophical theism, for the rest, to Unitarianism.

The various and inconsistent types of thought that are grouped together under the title of deism were alike in their errors rather than in what truths they attained. Their history and psychology of religion were in all cases false. They ignored the person and work of Christ. Their Christianity was Christless. They possessed more light than heat, and what heat they exhibited was in the anti-Christian aspect of the controversy. The movement ran dry in the sands of a barren rationalism. Perhaps the best indication of the defects of deism is found in the history of the movement itself, with its short-lived strength and utter collapse. Deism was stifled in the new atmosphere introduced by Methodism, rather than pierced by the cool logic of Butler. It afforded no ground for the religious needs or aspirations of man. It partook of the very aloofness it attributed to God. Such appeal as it possessed was rational, never emotional, and the new emotions raised in the breasts of the friends and opponents of Methodism, drew from deism such interest as it still held. Deism was dead before Wesley died.

Apart from the historical sense, deism is a term used to denote an attitude, which though not fully or directly maintained by any particular sect or party, has often been in evidence in various quarters. In this sense, it stands for the view that God created the world on a physical and according to some, moral basis, and left it to work according to fixed laws remaining wholly transcendent. In this connotation of the term, many religious systems have exhibited deistic features. Stoicism was, despite its pantheistic features, deistic in its conception of divine law and human morality. The indigenous religious systems of China are markedly deistic, whilst Islam, in its stress on the absoluteness of God, reveals an aspect much more reminiscent of deism than of theism.

The temper of some scientific men at the present day strikes a deistic note, and such rationalism as is not definitely agnostic is also deist. In this sense, deism is not a school so much as an

God and the World

attitude of thought, the temper which, whilst admitting God's existence, ignores any implications thereof. All over-emphasis of transcendence as naturally inclines to deism, as over-emphasis of immanence to pantheism. It is possible that the theology of Barth may take a deistic aspect in its development, at least in the hands of some of its expositors.

Since, however, the deistic spirit is ultimately subversive of all the values of religion, the deistic element in historical religions has usually been counterbalanced by other factors. It affords no place for worship, prayer or communion with God. The moral law is as much or as little an expression of His nature as the multiplication table. Deism is unfitted to be a religion. It is mechanistic, abstract, dualistic. In it God is reduced to a principle of explanation, at best to a demiurge. There is no link between God and man. Deism may be a philosophical theory, but even as such has small utility. As a religion it fails utterly, and that is why deism has been left high and dry by the tide of thought which has receded far from it.

Monotheistic Doctrines of God

If we define monotheism as belief in one and only one God, it is needful to relate the term to the other theories of the nature of the divine which have already been considered. Monotheism necessarily stands opposed to polytheism and to dualism of the theological type. It is possible to harmonize both monistic and pluralistic views with it. Deism is monotheistic. Theism, though technically not the same as monotheism, has virtually become so, although to the Jew and to the Muhammadan Christianity appears theistic rather than monotheistic, since both consider it has compromised its monotheism by the doctrine of the Trinity. Pantheism might claim to be a monotheistic creed, but it lacks that emphasis on the 'otherness' of God which characterizes ordinary monotheistic faith.

Historically, monotheism on the ethical side is the heritage of the world from the Hebrew prophets, and on the philosophical, it represents the development, in Christian hands, of the theism of the greater Greek thinkers, in whose case a distinction between theism and monotheism proper may be fitting. Semitic religion was characteristically henotheistic in its earlier stages, that is to say, each tribe worshipped its own

The Philosophical Approach to Religion

god, whilst recognizing that other peoples had gods of their own. To these, upon patriotic rather than on religious grounds, they owed no allegiance. From that basis the Jews, alone, apparently, of Semitic peoples, developed the idea of their God, Jahveh, as the only God, and drew the corollary that other gods were non-existent. Both Christianity and Islam derived their monotheism from them'

The claim that, long before Israel, Aken-Haten in Egypt, and Zoroaster in Iran, attained monotheism, is one that can be supported only by assumption from the paucity of the facts. It is antecedently unlikely that at those periods and amongst those nations anything more than henotheism would develop. Both these men showed an interest in and zeal for their own gods which excluded any mention of others. In the case of Aken-Haten, the relapse to polytheism was complete and speedy as soon as that monarch died. It is true that the Gathas, attributed to the prophet Zoroaster, know no god but Ahura Mazda, but they represent only a fragment of the religious literature of ancient Persia, and later development of ideas which are inherent in the Gathas themselves fully justified the impression of the Greeks that the system was radically dualistic. The claim that the Jew was the first true monotheist is not seriously challenged by the possibility, unproven if not unprovable, that others anticipated his creed. At least it may be said that even if they did, they failed to transmit their discovery.

Monotheism, of course, is not a religion, but an aspect of the higher religions. Apart from the common idea that God is one and that there is none beside Him, the monotheistic religions have no other doctrines that are uniform in them all. But a monotheistic faith will always be found to have some definite doctrine of God's relation to the world, as regards creation-providence, and also as regards the transcendence or immanence of God concerning that creation, and to these points we can now turn.

THE IDEA OF CREATION

ANDREW LANG once remarked that as soon as man made things himself he would be ready to think of a Maker of things. Certainly the origins of the idea of creation go back further than any historical records can carry us, and the testimony of

God and the World

human thought at all stages favours the notion that the world is the work of some creative power, rather than that itself is an eternally existent actuality. In primitive thought totem animals or wizards are sometimes named as creators. In other cases creation is the work of 'high gods'. At the polytheistic stage the myths often attribute creation to the union of earth and sky gods, or at times to a demiurge. The last stage of pre-Christian thought is found in the philosophical systems of Greece, though they were antedated by Indian philosophy. In the days when Greek thought was dawning, Gotama the Buddha had already discouraged speculation as to the causes of things as profitless, a fact which suggests that Indian philosophy had worked itself to a standstill upon the subject.

Christian thought inherited the orthodox Jewish dogma of creation *ex nihilo*, which at any rate enabled it to avoid the dualism of a creator and the 'stuff' out of which he creates. Moreover, *ex nihilo*, need not mean more than that creation proceeds from the divine mind in the way that from our minds may come a mental image of that which is non-existent. It serves to insist on the 'soleness' of God, and on the dependence of all things on Him alone. Both Jewish and Christian thinkers found it by no means easy to reconcile Genesis with Aristotle in this respect, and many were the ingenious contrivances by which the two authorities were made to sing in tune.

Later, from the more strictly philosophical standpoint, the crux of the matter began to be found in the relation of God to the time process. Is creation within time? If so, is God within time? Or was time created with the universe?

Some answer to these difficulties at least is found in regarding creation not as an act, but as an activity, as the manifestation of that self-activity which is the life of God, of which the universe is but one aspect. A view that was held by Origen cannot be called new, and one that appealed to the acute mind of Erigena cannot be called a mere evasion of the problem. Augustine held that the preservation of the universe amounted to a continuous creation. Aquinas, who felt obliged to accept the notion of a beginning of all things, despaired of any demonstration of the fact, and referred it to that faith which was so often useful to him in removing, or in this case in creating, mountains. In modern times the view has found many de-

The Philosophical Approach to Religion

fenders, including T. H. Green, who regarded the world and God as necessary to each other, as subject and object. This view makes no contribution to the difficulties of relating time and God, but to us who are immersed in time as the fish in the sea, it is virtually impossible to have any idea upon such a subject that is not in some respect either self-contradictory or unintelligible, even if only because we can have no real conception of the significance of the term eternity in its relation to time. To speak of an eternal process of creation raises that question, and that is why it is better to call it an activity, and leave aside the question of the relation of divine activity to our temporal order, for at any rate we can hardly assume that such an activity is wholly absorbed in it.

As regards the universe, we may accept the testimony of Sir J. H. Jeans, who says, 'Everything points with overwhelming force to a definite event or series of events of creation, at some time or times not infinitely remote. The universe cannot have originated by chance out of its present ingredients, and neither can it have always been the same as now' (*Eos*, p. 55). This judgement is based upon the fact that the atoms which compose the universe are in a state of radiation which implies that they are dissolving, and cannot be eternal. Hence the remark that the universe is like a clock running down, with no one to rewind it. Jeans concedes the possibility of Millikan's hypothesis of the renewal of the universe, without acknowledging that it can be more than an unlikely one. The chances of two stars coming near enough to tear each other apart and set up another solar system are so remote that he calls our solar system a freak or cosmic accident. He estimates the age of the earth as 2,000 million years. Some idea of the relative value of this figure is given when we realize that light from the most distant objects visible takes 140 million years to reach us. Jeans calculates that the earth can provide a home for mankind for some million million years. Such calculations, of course, are highly speculative. We cannot be certain that solar heat radiates in all directions equally. If it does not, these figures would be vastly increased. Others, assuming that the interior of the earth contains radio-active substances, prophesy that it will be caused long before this to melt by fervent heat, owing to their disintegration.

God and the World

Such views, of course, have no particular bearing on the idea that creation is a continuous activity, of which this universe is but one event. We have referred already to views like those of Whitehead which reject the idea of God as a creator in the ordinary sense, and those of Alexander that in the beginning was space-time and in the end will be God. The modern conception of space-time is necessary to provide a background for a philosophy that deals not with a physical universe mentally apprehended, but with a universe that is a system of 'events'. Space-time is the screen on which events are projected, but the concept of space-time, whilst useful in this and other ways, raises philosophical questions as to the relation of both to God, for space-time is, after all, by itself no easier to conceive than Newton's empty space and flowing time. Time applies to the thought-process as space does not, and for that reason can never be treated by philosophy as always hyphenated with space. There is a temporal relation entirely distinguishable from the spatial relation even for physics, and this must have a connexion with the time of consciousness, which the spatial relation does not possess. After all, thought, even in the mind of God, seems to imply a relation to time that it does not bear to space, just as our thought does. The problem of the relation of the creative process to time resolves itself therefore into the wider issue of the relation of the divine consciousness to time, and that, as we have said, is one that can hardly be solved by our minds. Any theistic philosophy, however, which attributes reality to human experience seems necessarily to imply that at least in so far as God enters into the life of man, his consciousness enters into the time relation, though that need not imply that it is subject to time in the manner our consciousness must be.

THE IDEA OF PROVIDENCE

THOUGH the care of the creator for creation is a thought common to most religions, and one that appeared strongly in Stoic philosophy, which identified God and Providence, the main development of the idea of Providence is Biblical and Christian. The term providence, which often serves as an impersonal title of the Deity, is never referred to God in the Bible. It is applied

The Philosophical Approach to Religion

in the book of the Wisdom of Solomon to the forethought of God, and in the New Testament twice to human care and forethought. Nevertheless, the idea of Providence runs throughout the Old and New Testaments. In the hands of the schoolmen it was made the subject of many fine distinctions, such as universal, general, particular, special and most special providences. To the teleological theology of Paley's day, the various adaptations of Nature were manifest marks of providence. The mood of modern thought, in reaction, seems inclined to admit only general and not special providence, though if this imply that divine care omits the individual, it is a poor conception of the God who though He is high, yet has respect unto the lowly, for the true sign of God's greatness is that it is able to regard the least.

The conception of Providence must necessarily be related to the ideas that are accepted of God's omnipotence, and man's freedom, and also to the question of His immanence and transcendence in the world. But some doctrine of providence is inevitable in any theistic, as contrasted with a deistic, conception of God, for the problems of providence are those of theism generally, and it is for this reason that it is needless to pursue the question separately here. It has already been said that the responsiveness of God to human needs is the *sine quâ non* of religious faith of every kind, and to that extent providence is a universal conception of religion. The question at stake is not that of providence or none, but of the extent and working of that providence, and the answer which will be given to that will be manifest in the whole treatment of our conception of God and man.

IMMANENCE AND TRANSCENDENCE

THE antithesis between immanence and transcendence is comparatively recent, but the actual issue runs back to the beginnings of theistic thought, and its extreme phases are revealed in the doctrines of deism and pantheism.

A thorough-going doctrine of immanence must lead to pantheism, and in order to avoid that extreme it is needful to recognize degrees of immanence, in something like the manner in which F. H. Bradley conceived of degrees of reality. The

God and the World

external world, animate nature, and the spirit of man, may be said to represent differing degrees of such immanence. It was on account of the pantheistic tendency of the doctrine that Martineau declared God to be immanent in nature but not in man, thus reversing the view of Jacobi, who said that God was present to man through the heart just as Nature was through the senses, yet added, 'there is light in my heart, but when I seek to bring it to the understanding, it is extinguished'. For this reason he confessed himself 'a heathen with the understanding, but a Christian with the spirit'.

Alike with immanence and transcendence, the extreme assertion always results in a conception of God that proves dangerous to theism. The emphasis on transcendence which some of the older theologies, such as Calvanism, manifested, was in some degree set off by the ideas of providence and miraculous intervention of God in the world of man. It served at least to assert the divine sovereignty, and that sense of the 'otherness' of God which in some degree belongs to all forms of religion that are not pantheistic or deeply mystical. Now that the safeguards of a miraculous providence are not much in evidence, there is some danger that the modern conception of transcendence may work towards a new form of deism. The nineteenth century tended to stress the idea of immanence, and gave signs of a reaction towards a more sharply defined conception of the transcendence of God, of which Otto and Barth are now symptomatic. The doctrine of immanence which came as the reaction of the nineteenth century against the deism of the eighteenth has led to the quickened interest in mysticism which has characterized the past generation. Now the pendulum seems to be swinging slowly in the opposite direction.

It is difficult to say which conception, taken alone, immanence or transcendence, is the more apt to mislead. We do not guard against pantheism merely by asserting that the immanent God is also transcendent, for such transcendence is apt to be altogether uncharacterized, and merely a formal acknowledgement to allay suspicion of pantheism. It is only by a definite doctrine of divine personality that a complete answer to pantheism can come, and yet it is that very doctrine which is imperilled by radical conceptions of immanence. If theism is to avoid this

The Philosophical Approach to Religion

Scylla and Charybdis, some definite partition between immanence and transcendence is necessary, and it must be said in what way both belong to God. Perhaps the best way is by stressing the moral distinction between man and God, the reality of human evil, and man's responsibility for it. The immanence of God in man, therefore, is limited by man's sin, and the divine transcendence is moral rather than simply the transcendence of the infinite over the finite. In such manner it is possible to mark out the spheres of God and man in the moral realm, and secure that degree of transcendence which guards against pantheism without resorting to a conception that leads towards deism.

Chapter VIII

God and Man

REASON AND REVELATION

The Conception of 'Natural Theology'
THE question of the divine-human relationship from the standpoint of philosophy introduces first of all the much-debated issue of the source of man's knowledge of God, whether it comes through reason or revelation. Thomas Aquinas made a sharp separation between the spheres of natural and revealed theology. He did not deny that reason had a place in religion, but regarded it as deficient rather than deceptive. By its light man cannot fully grasp God, and faith enters to supplement, not destroy, reason. Reason may give truths also given by revelation, but what reason gives is not the articles of the faith, but rather a kind of prolegomena to them.

The idea of natural theology was an attractive ground for speculation, since it was necessarily held that, when man was created, his mind could not have been wholly destitute of ideas of a general and also of a theological character. So it came to be supposed that man had a 'natural' religion and that natural theology would be found in certain rational beliefs deducible from the nature of man and the universe. Lord Herbert of Cherbury, brother of the poet, published in 1624, a century before the deist movement, his *Tractatus de Veritate*, in which he stated what he believed to be the universal ideas belonging to the mind of mankind. He included in them the five 'common notions' (*communes notitiae*) of natural religion:

(1) There is a God;
(2) He should be worshipped;
(3) Worship lies particularly in piety and virtue;
(4) Repentance is necessary;
(5) A future life of reward or punishment exists.

The notion of natural theology was not necessarily opposed

to the idea of revelation, it being usually held that, whilst natural theology represented such ideas as man possessed by reason of his making, a specific revelation was granted subsequently through the prophets, and finally in the Christian dispensation. It was the deists and the deistically-minded who stressed the antithesis. The only Christian thinker of note before Kant who accepted revelation and denied spiritual insight to reason was Bacon, who was neither clear nor consistent in the matter. Kant's limitation of reason was counterbalanced by his stress on 'practical reason' or conscience, as God's only authentic revelation, though he accepted the Bible as interpreted thereby and showed no little interest in theological questions. Mansel's attempt to deny reason for revelation has been mentioned earlier, and seems to have been directed towards proving the necessity of the Church, but such legacy as Mansel left was claimed by the sceptics, not by believers.

The controversy flamed up afresh in the storms of the 'science and religion' debates of the nineteenth century, when Gladstone, from 'the impregnable rock of Holy Scripture', defied Huxley. But when Christian theology lost its fear of the doctrine of evolution, and when the comparative study of religion showed ideas of God that in many respects bore comparison with our own, were found in other faiths, the whole position altered. Man was no longer thought to have necessarily received any primitive revelation as the only means of explaining why he had an idea of the divine, and the claims of natural theology, obsolescent long before this, disappeared altogether. But at the same time, the conception of reason and its function was altering also, and in this twofold way the whole antithesis of reason and revelation was entirely modified.

The Meaning of Revelation

Revelation once denoted the Bible from cover to cover. It is now admitted that, in a sense, all knowledge is revelation—'a man can receive nothing except it be given him from heaven'. This seems specially true of our ideals, and those flashes of deep insight of which we often say 'it came to me'.

Revelation is a psychological process. There are degrees of

God and Man

spiritual insight, and the application or extension of common truths by men of the spirit is as much revelation as any direct or new message. Revelation is not passively received. 'He that seeketh findeth,' which implies that knowledge depends on search, and revelation needs active reception to be effective. The modern conception of revelation is rather that of intercourse between God and man in which God gives and man receives, according to his ability and effort. The old idea was like that of Muhammad's Qu'ran, the outpouring of truth into a passive recipient.

The comparative study of religion has taught us to see some revelation in all forms of belief. The critical study of scripture has modified the mechanical notion of uniform inspiration, attaching itself to the book as a whole. Revelation means today that human knowledge is a gift from God. It may be asked, therefore, are the Beatitudes revealed in the same degree and manner as the theory of relativity? The answer is that the one is a matter of spiritual, the other of intellectual insight. While both may be called revelation, yet the appreciation of the one depends upon conditions that are open to all who have spiritual minds, the other can be appreciated only by the learned. It is equally true that only a good man could have conceived the Beatitudes, only a learned man the theory of relativity. In the latter, therefore, the human brain and its knowledge are specifically in evidence, in the former the divine factor is more prominent, and that is why we regard the term 'revealed' as more aptly applied to the one than to the other.

The Function of Reason

Reference has already been made to Kant's contention that pure reason was incapable, from its very nature, of giving God, freedom or immortality. Kant's epistemology, which was a veritable thunderbolt to the eighteenth century, has not only lost some of its basis, but much of its terrors. It remains that Kant was right, if any one thinks that a scientific demonstration of these things is possible; but as not even the nature of the reality with which science deals can be demonstrated in this way, there is less reason for alarm that the nature of God is incapable of such demonstration. In neither case is reason debarred from going as far as it can. It is no longer possible to imagine that God is a projection of man's own thought, whilst science deals with objective reality, for the atom is as much a projection as the idea of God, differing only in that certain sense evidence is possible regarding its track. Yet no man has seen or even imagined an atom. It represents something that is assumed by virtue of certain evidence, but Robinson Crusoe had a great deal more evidence by which to imagine the cause of the footprint he saw than we have to imagine, from what we might liken to the footprints of the atom, what manner of reality it represents. The actual being of the atom, if it can be said to have a being, is as much a mystery as the being of God.

Moreover, quite apart from our realization of such limitations of reason, we are now, thanks to modern psychology, more able to judge its character and the part it has played in human evolution. Genetic psychology has shown that reason is instrumental rather than critical and impartial, and intimately connected with conation. In theory, feeling and will are subjective, reason objective. Yet in practice, the conflict of theories and policies, all supported by reason, shows how precarious is the assumed objectivity of reason. It is only purely abstract reasoning, like that of mathematics, which is wholly objective; when reason is applied to practical problems it loses much of its objective character and becomes the instrument for justifying and furthering the ends conation seeks. That is why so much reasoning is really 'rationalization'.

The Relation of Reason and Revelation

What has been said explains why the old contrast of reason and revelation has lost its point. Whatever is revealed must be proportionate to and in harmony with reason, which is the 'candle of the Lord' within a man. An alleged revelation inherently contradictory must sooner or later collapse, despite the claims made on behalf of the Qu'ran, or by our own Fundamentalists. This does not mean that whatever is set forth in the name of revelation must be capable of rational proof or even of rational understanding. The Sermon on the Mount, for example, would not answer this demand, and

God and Man

yet there is nothing in it which is unreasonable or offends our intellect.

At the same time, though reason judges revelation, revelation, or spiritual insight, judges reason. We no longer quote Scripture against science, but we can and should use the Sermon on the Mount against theories of man, society and morality which conflict with it.

The restricted claims for revelation, which is no longer called upon to guarantee the irrational and incredible as true, and equally the restricted claims for reason, which no longer can pose as an impartial critical faculty, have alike served to solve the old conflict between revealed and so-called natural theology. It was once asked how men could have gained spiritual knowledge unless it was revealed, and even those who rejected the Christian revelation had to assume some revelation given to the first man, from which he derived his natural religion. The theory of evolution set all this aside, and the conceptions of reason and revelation meet in the philosophy of religion to-day, without suggesting any necessary conflict.

The term revelation means either the process or the result of revealing, and reason usually denotes what is logically consistent. We believe in revelation if we hold God makes known to man spiritual and moral truth. If we hold also that such knowledge must be consistent with our moral and spiritual sense and our reason, it is because we hold the latter is also the gift of God. One of God's gifts will not conflict with another. Hence reason and revelation are complementary and not antagonistic processes.

THE RELATION OF GOD TO HUMANITY

Creation and Limitation

THE early Church accepted the Hebrew notion that God created the body and soul of man, and hence Plato's views about the pre-existence of spirits were made unorthodox. Indeed, this was one of the reasons why Plato was cast aside into neglect, when the much less spiritual philosophy of Aristotle was esteemed by the Church. If we accept the idea of creation as a continuous process, the notion of the eternal existence of spirits seems to follow, since an eternally creative process would imply that something was eternally created, and that 'something' can hardly be thought of as non-spiritual in character. On the other hand, the close association of body and soul favours the idea of the creation of the soul that is connected with each separate body. An eternal society of spirits deriving its existence from God, is not an anti-theistic notion, indeed it has been the teaching of many pluralists in philosophy. It was held by Origen and Erigena. The orthodox dogma of creationism was supported by Jerome, Anselm, and Aquinas, whilst Tertullian favoured traducianism, i.e. the doctrine that the soul was inherited from the parents, in the same manner as the body. Despite the objection of certain mediaeval divines that if God created a separate soul to inhabit the body, it compelled Him to give souls to the illegitimately born, the creationist idea prevailed and is now one of those dogmas that are accepted without question by the majority of Christians, the more readily, of course, since the practical issues are not particularly important whatever way we think on such a matter.

Since we lack the knowledge that would enable us to hold any definite opinion on such a subject, it is better to regard it as an open question. Most will think it natural that a new soul should enter into existence with a new body, but the East has long thought otherwise, and though the empirical evidence for transmigration is very precarious, the belief should not be summarily dismissed. Moreover, many of the arguments that bear upon immortality can work backwards towards pre-existence as well as forwards to existence after this life.

Of much greater importance is the question of what Pringle-Pattison once called the almost insuperable difficulty of finding room for God and man in the universe. If man has a 'substantival' existence, not an 'adjectival', that is to say, if he is an independent personality, not a 'mode' of God, it is argued that God is limited by such an existence other than His own, and therefore finite. One cannot help the impression that a great deal of what has been written upon this subject owes much to prejudice aroused by the term 'a finite God'. To press the word finite strictly, certainly implies a conception of God

God and Man

that does scant justice to Him. Yet equally to press the term infinite results in a conception of God that either removes Him out of all touch with man, or reduces the existence of man to a mere shadow of his Creator. In any case both terms, finite and infinite, are bound to have a meaning that cannot be the same when applied to the divine existence as when applied to human notions. As said (p. 101), the term infinite, in any other than its mathematical connotation, is negatively used as the denial of the characteristics of the finite. If we speak of God as finite, it need not mean finite in the sense in which we are finite, and that for two reasons.

The first is that in any case man cannot be wholly independent of God. Even Leibniz's monads, each self-contained and independent of the rest, depended upon the supreme monad, God, who created them and arranged their pre-established harmony. Lotze, who maintained the real existence of human souls, held that God served as the principle of interaction between them. Man is finite because he is dependent upon God, but God is not finite in any such sense, for He does not depend upon man. Secondly, whatever limitation is placed upon the divine nature by the existence of man with power of self-determination, is a self-imposed limitation on the part of God, which cannot be equated with the limitations imposed upon us by other than our choice. The universe might be likened to the 'body' of God, because it is for Him what our bodies are for us, the means of His self-manifestation. Within that universe arise human beings who seem to possess the power to manifest in themselves that which is not the will of God. It cannot be denied that, in some sense, God must be limited in His self-expression by such actions, yet none other than God can have chosen it so, and surely the omnipotence of God must be as free to limit as to assert itself. An omnipotence that could not choose its own conditions would be a contradiction in terms. Looked at from that standpoint, the term finite loses its suggestion of imperfection when applied to God. Whichever way we view the problem, the difficulties are serious. Experience presents us with an in-dyed pluralism, from which we cannot shake ourselves. Our monism is purely theoretical. We think and act as pluralists. The indubitable sense of personal reality is the most fundamental fact of experience. We are told that such a reality cannot actually be. The only reality is God. In the interests of guarding the supremacy of God, we are to deny the fact of our own existence. If there is one thing that is certain in experience, it is our own sense of existence. We believe in the existence of God, for our own experience introduces us to something greater than itself, and no man who knows himself and life, can doubt that other reality. Yet he may not even call it God, and none can be certain of the full characteristics of a nature that so transcends his own. It seems, therefore, a poor reason for doing injustice to the fact of our known human nature to argue that its reality must be denied, or at least so qualified as to make it but a passing shadow on the surface of an eternal unchanging background, because a human conception of the divine nature, a conception which changes with the changes of thought, lays it down that it is inadmissible to treat God as limited by His creation. Jesus, at any rate, who knew God as none other has ever known Him, was not oppressed by the almost insuperable difficulty of finding room for God and man. That difficulty belongs to philosophy rather than to religion, and philosophy will be wise in seeing that it respects experience sufficiently to find room for man, even if it leave to God the task of manifesting His own place in His scheme of things.

THE PROBLEM OF EVIL

TO say that the problem of evil is insoluble is not an excuse for burking it, nor does it mean that there is no solution. It is insoluble in the sense that an equation is insoluble when insufficient data are provided for working it out. The unknown factor in this case is the reason for the existence of man upon earth. If this were known, the problem might present no difficulty. As it is unknown, we can do no more than conjecture, and little can be said that has not been said and said again.

To the present day, pain presents a more frequent obstacle than sin, in contrast to the Middle Ages, which, with a much greater experience of suffering than we have, thought less of it than of sin. The idea of nature as a struggle for existence, the 'dismal cockpit' of Huxley's phrase, oppressed the Victorians,

God and Man

and still obsesses many minds. Yet both Darwin and Wallace denied that such was a correct picture of animal evolution. A wild animal suffers a minimal quantity of pain and fear. No one who has watched a bird feeding can hold that his ceaseless alertness, his never-ending guard against his enemies, spoils his happiness. The misery of fear to us is that we think fear. The bird does not, and his caution is in no sense unpleasant to him, for actual fear comes only in the face of imminent danger. As W. H. Hudson, the closest of observers of bird life has said, the bird is never miserable. When death comes, if it come from another animal, the butchers of the Wild are swift and humane killers, and if it comes naturally, the passage from life to death in wild nature, as Hudson says, is swift and easy. The values of the spur of pain in physical evolution need not be mentioned, and since the bitterness of both suffering and death lies in the thought of it, the animals know little of that darker side of the problem of pain that oppresses us. No natural process is really painful, and to die is, after all, as natural as to be born.

When we pass to the human side of the question, some of the values of pain in physical evolution remain, and certain spiritual values are added. At any rate, the removal of pain would remove many of the virtues associated with it, pity, patience, longsuffering, endurance, bravery, and so forth. This is not to say that the reason for suffering lies in these things, but merely to afford a reminder that there are compensations, and that the problem must not be presented in colours too dark.

Although, as we have said, it is not possible to suggest a reason for the sufferings of existence, another question arises as to the compatibility of the existence of suffering with a belief in a good God, and that question can be answered.

In the first place, we have no other reason for calling pain an evil than our own strong dislike of it, but there is no ground for assuming that what is unwelcome to us must thereby be shown to be, in any ultimate sense, bad. Certainly, the fact of pain shows that there is a conflict between the nature which our Maker has given us, and the conditions under which He has set us to live, but that does not necessarily imply that He is not good, or that pain must be ultimately bad, especially if we recall that a great deal of what we suffer is the result of our altering the conditions of life as originally given.

In the second place, belief in the goodness and power of God grew up in face of the known fact of pain. Actually, therefore, that fact was unable to prevent the belief from arising and being maintained. To say it is fatal to that belief is simply untrue. It is not. One can argue that it should be fatal to it, but that is altogether another question, and the answer of the vast majority of those who have suffered most, and who should therefore be better able to appreciate the issue than the mere theorist, is that actual experience of suffering far more often strengthens belief than injures it. Such an indisputable fact is worth pondering by those whose theory is that suffering should destroy our faith in God's goodness.

Indeed, the problem of pain can be maintained as a problem only so long as belief in God is also maintained. If there is no good God, pain remains as an unwelcome fact, but no longer as a problem. It follows that the problem exists only for those who hold the belief, and the fact that they continue to believe shows that they have not found the problem, at any rate in practice, as damaging as the critics of theism think. The fact of pain may serve as an explanation of an individual's own unwillingness to believe in a good God, but his refusal to believe removes the problem as far as he is concerned, and he may be well advised to allow others to face in their own way a problem that concerns them and not him.

Moral evil or sin presents even greater difficulties than does pain. It is possible to contend that pain is not wholly an evil, but this cannot be the case with regard to sin. Some, for example, have thought that it may be held that God suffers, but none can think God sins, and this fact alone is enough to show the difference between the two kinds of evil, the physical and the moral.

Yet for the same reason as was mentioned in the case of pain, the fact of sin does not contradict belief in God. Indeed, to a large extent belief in God was the cause of the recognition of sin as what it is. Without the law, St. Paul said, he had not known sin. The attempt to utilize the fact of sin to deny the existence of a good God suffers from the same disability that we saw attached to the similar attempt with regard to pain.

God and Man

Without the belief in God, there would have been no belief in sin. It is no coincidence that the Hebrew race, with the deepest insight of any of the peoples of antiquity regarding the character of God, also possessed the liveliest sense of sin. The problem of sin is scarcely entertained at the lowest stages of spiritual development. It enters and increases with the stages of higher spiritual apprehension.

If we ask why sin is sin, why wrong wrong, we are brought to see how naturally and inevitably we believe that what is right and good should exist. There is no problem of goodness, only of evil. Those, therefore, who put forward the objection that moral evil is a contradiction of theistic belief must find themselves in a curious position. They assert that there is no good God, and yet in order to assert that there is not, they must take up the position that there should be such a Being, for sin cannot be an objection unless it is assumed that the Good should exist. They therefore occupy the same ground as the believer as far as testimony to the essential rights of the Good to exist are concerned. Only they are in the unsatisfactory position of believing in good which has no basis in the universe, whilst the theist believes that good is based in the very nature of reality.

Whatever way we look at the matter, it must appear that the ground of the universe, and of our own existence, whether we call that ground God or not, has produced alike both the conditions which allow the appearance of evil and those which allow us to condemn and fight against it. If the former appearance of evil is quoted as evidence against the goodness of God, the latter fighting it affords equally good evidence against His moral impotence or neutrality. Why a being morally indifferent, to whom good and bad are alike just phases of the world process, should create beings who are so profoundly affected where he is neutral is just as serious a problem as why a good God who hates evil should permit it. We do not escape difficulties, therefore, by rejecting theism. We only exchange them. It may be a question of temperament and training which side of the difficulty seems less to us, but it is impossible to saddle theism with the problem of evil. To those who do not believe in God there is, of course, no problem of reconciling evil with divine goodness, but there is the insoluble enigma why from the same world ground should come good and bad, and why we should be so constituted as to be passionately partisan in a conflict in which allegedly the world ground from which we sprang is neutral and indifferent.

Chapter IX
Immortality

Early Beliefs

THE belief that death is not the cessation of existence is in some sense characteristic of every form of religion, and probably as old at least as animism. Evidence from burials affords traces of the belief as far back as the palaeolithic age. Though there is considerable difference regarding the state of the dead as conceived in various historical faiths, the idea of survival is common to all. Not even Buddhism can be quoted as anomalous, for, apart altogether from the high probability that its original teaching accepted the idea of a soul, or at least of the essential man as surviving death, it remains that, even according to the modern presentation, karma survives and forms a new existence. The reaction that led to doubt of survival and to desire for non-existence is not primitive. The Veda does not recognize transmigration, nor exhibit any of that weariness of life that appears in the later developments of Brahmanism.

Plato affords the first example of philosophical appreciation of the significance of the idea of the survival of the soul after death, and in his dialogues we are provided with the arguments that form the first theoretical essay in belief in immortality. In *Meno* we find the traditional character of the belief; in *Timaeus* he deals with the soul's divine origin and transmigration; in the *Republic* he argues the soul can overcome the attacks of the 'disease' of sin and therefore may be assumed to be able to overcome death, since, on the analogy of the body, a man who can overcome all diseases would be immortal. At the close of the book is the myth of Er the Armenian, in which he gives us a vivid picture of his conception of survival in the after-life. In *Phaedrus* he argues that the soul had a prior existence in which it had known the Ideas, and hence was able to recognize in this existence their earthly copies, knowledge being 'anamnesis' (that is, recollection). The *Symposium* deals with the present, and the *Phaedo* with the after-existence, of the soul.

The Philosophical Approach to Religion

The Platonic arguments can be summed up as follows. They insist first of all on moral retribution. In heaven or hell, man receives according as his works have been. Plato, however, is cautious and undogmatic, stating expressly that he spoke in allegory, and while he regarded his doctrine as true in spirit, he did not wish it to be pressed in the letter. His arguments stress the indestructibility of the soul, and although this is applied in some cases to prove its pre-existence rather than after-existence, those which deal with the soul's ideals and aims and the moral need for another life are still powerful. On the other side, some of Plato's arguments seem childish to-day; others lose their point with the rejection of his doctrine of Ideas; others are 'over-beliefs' in which Plato expresses speculations regarding the demiurge, the total number of souls, and their relations to the stars, which Plato thought were alive. Then, also, Plato accepted from Pythagoras the notion of transmigration, and he was as interested in pre-existence as in survival. Finally, he disparaged the body, and was interested in immortality for philosophers and not for the many.

Although the intellectual interest overrides the moral, and Plato's philosophy rather than his religion made him believe in immortality, it remains true that these arguments represent the highest point which was reached by the ancient world until the teaching of Christ.

Later Development of the Idea of Immortality

Philosophical interest in the idea of immortality owes its revival very largely to Kant, who regarded it as essential to religion. He gave the following definition: 'The immortality of the soul means the infinitely prolonged existence and personality of one and the same rational being,' a definition that does not cover the immortality of the soul as such, but rather its rational aspect, and some might argue that it could not be applied to the immortality of, shall we say, the young child, unless we understood the child to be a potentially rational being. Kant, however, distinguishes immortality from survival, since survival of death need not be infinitely prolonged.

The view of Spinoza, Schleiermacher, and some of the mystics that the individual is a 'mode' or part of the Absolute, and the view that man is immortal simply in his influence on and legacy

Immortality

to the race (like the Hebrew idea of immortality in one's 'seed') are both indistinguishable in actual effect from annihilation. The material world may be called a mode of God, and so immortal. With regard to the second view, the midge eaten by the swallow leaves its legacy to the race of living creatures, and apparently, therefore, is in that sense, immortal. If it is replied that spirit is immortal in a sense in which material things cannot be, it makes no radical difference, for the spirit lost in God as the river in the sea, loses its identity. The only meaning we can attach to the word annihilation is loss of identity. Strictly speaking, we cannot conceive the annihilation of existence. Such views as these are misleading in that they try to attach the values of immortality to a state which in no intelligent sense can be called the eternal persistence of the soul's identity.

Objections to the Idea of Immortality

Objections to the idea of immortality fall into two main classes, with various sub-divisions. The first class consists of those who contend that there is not sufficient evidence to assume anything concerning the soul after death. Dr. Broad has suggested that just as the body remains for a while after death before its final disintegration, so may it be with the spirit. He thinks spiritistic phenomena may be thus explained, especially since 'messages' seem to come more frequently from those who have recently died than from those who have been dead for a long while. Since there is no particular reason beyond these for the theory, it cannot be said to be strongly based. But it serves as a reminder that survival and immortality are not the same thing.

Turning, however, to the complaint of lack of evidence generally, the previous question is what type of evidence is required. 'If they hear not Moses and the prophets, neither will they be persuaded though one rose from the dead.' For those who want it, spiritism professes to offer evidence of the senses, but to expect that what is ultimately real must be demonstrable to physical sense is to beg the question. Even the ultimate nature of the physical world is not of a character that can be estimated by sense perception.

Evidence, however, can be offered by the cumulative testimony of converging lines of argument. Of such evidence there

The Philosophical Approach to Religion

is plenty. It may not be accepted, but it is gratuitous to object that evidence is lacking, when the only sort of evidence which seems possible is present in sufficient degree to have convinced the greatest thinkers of the world from Plato to Kant of the reality of the after-life. Objections grounded on lack of evidence therefore amount to the demand that a certain kind of evidence, which in the nature of the case cannot be afforded, shall be the only evidence received.

There is no doubt that some who argue that there is no evidence do not desire that there should be. A few have frankly admitted this. Harriet Martineau expressly desired that death should be the utter end of her, declaring that this life in itself was sufficient both in its good and bad. Such cases are rare. Historically, it is certain that the mass of mankind, from primitive times down, have earnestly desired future life, and every religion without exception has endorsed that desire. Apart from a few theorists, the bulk of those who find the thought of the after-life repugnant, are the worldly who in this life only have hope, and to whom any spiritual existence seems as undesirable as the shadowy Hades to the life-loving Greeks, or Sheol to the Jew. The exceptions are those who think the desire for individual after-life is egoistic. This may be a reaction from the old ideas of a reward for righteousness in Heaven, witness Paley's celebrated definition of virtue: 'doing good for the sake of everlasting happiness and in obedience to will of God.' One can understand the protest that good is intrinsically right here and now, whether or no its issues are carried over into another life. Some add to this the view mentioned above, that all the immortality we need is to live in the memory of the good we have done. Incidentally, one realizes that celebrated murderers live longer in the memory than most benefactors. William James discussed the 'tiresomeness of an overpeopled heaven' crowded with the Chinese! He dismissed the idea as 'a sign of human incapacity' to grasp, from our finite outlook, the pre-suppositions of an infinite and eternal existence.

The second type of objection is based on the supposed relation of mind to matter, and of thought to the physical brain. Despite the pertinacity of the materialistically-minded in dismissing consciousness, consciousness persists in returning. Huxley once admitted 'the appearance of consciousness as the result of

Immortality

irritating nervous tissues' to be as inexplicable as the appearance of the djinn when Aladdin rubbed his lamp. James Ward demonstrated clearly the untenability of regarding consciousness as an 'epiphenomenon', a superfluity in evolution whose arrival and survival are inexplicable, and none but the Behaviourists, and a few of the surviving fundamentalists of materialism, cling to this view to-day. The attempt to interpret the universe in terms of matter or energy breaks down utterly before the undeniable characteristics of living organisms.

The legacy of this type of objection has passed to those who argue from the fact that injury to the brain produces partial or complete amnesia, that the destruction of the brain at death must result in the utter disappearance of thought, and hence that death is the entire end of existence. Consciousness is a function of the brain, and without a brain to function there can be no consciousness. Such a view is superficially plausible, but it is after all the same as arguing that because we cut off the wireless the speaker has ceased to be able to speak. It is fortunate for broadcasters that it is otherwise.

Long ago, James distinguished permissible or transmissive function from productive function. The material world exhibits both. Heat applied to water produces steam, but the trigger does not in the same sense produce the explosion; it releases the constituent gases in the powder, and as they resume their normal bulk, that displacement of air occurs which we call an explosion. A prism does not produce the spectrum, but transmits the light and so exhibits it That the relation of the brain to thought should be of productive type is, said James, 'not a jot more simple or credible than any other conceivable theory', but 'only a little more popular'. A transmissive theory explains better the psychical phenomena such as telepathy, &c. As Kant said: 'The death of the body may indeed be the end of the sensational use of our mind, but only the beginning of the intellectual. The body would thus be not the cause of our thinking, but merely a condition restrictive thereof.'

Similarly we may deal with the objection that unconsciousness under anaesthetics suggests extinction at death. It certainly suspends memory, but memory survives the suspension. May it not then survive the interruption of death? At any rate, the argument from anaesthetics is one that will cut both ways.

The Philosophical Approach to Religion

It is difficult to avoid the conclusion that the question of immortality is regarded more from the affective than the rational standpoint, even when the professed ground is argumentative. Those who desire to believe, generally find arguments sufficient to justify them, and those who do not desire to believe, find sufficient ground for scepticism.

The Arguments for Immortality

We may summarize the chief philosophical arguments as follows, leaving aside such as belong to Scripture or Christian experience, and confining our attention solely to the philosophical issue to which our subject limits us.

(1) *The Teleological Argument.* This is based on life's incompleteness. We are potential rather than actual personalities. Every one who has developed the higher side of his nature realizes how much greater that side might be. The more he fulfils of what this life offers, the more he sees the still unexhausted possibilities of the spiritual life. This suggests a fuller function hereafter for the possibilities unexhausted in this life, according to the natural law which shows that the development of any power never exceeds its function, present or to come. Moral and spiritual powers do not fulfil any definite biological function in the narrower sense. They seem to be 'grown on earth for use in heaven'. Although in some part they are fulfilled here, they carry within themselves much more than this life can exhaust, and therefore the only meaning that can be attached to certain indications given by our present powers is that they are for use hereafter. The analogies drawn between animals and men dying alike, are vitiated by the fact that even here on earth man can transcend his environment, but an animal cannot. This, at any rate, suggests that he may be able so to transcend his environment ultimately as to survive the bodily dissolution and attain immortality.

(2) *The Moral Argument.* This represents another aspect of the preceding argument, the negative rather than the positive side of it. It refers to the injustice and the inequality of life—the lives hampered by sickness, the lives of the insane, the early death of children, and so on. It also points out that both evil and good often go unrecompensed in this life. The argument suggests there that this life demands a sequel, wherein justice

Immortality

will redistribute things and award to every man according to his work.

The positive side of this argument is that the moral law is the most absolute of all human convictions and has a strength that none of our intellectual beliefs possess. We have learned to disbelieve in many of the laws of the physical universe as they were taught us at school, but we cannot imagine ourselves becoming convinced that under any circumstances it is right to be selfish. If anything, then, be immortal in a changing world, it must be moral law. In this life the moral law often seems to lack vindication. Yet its absolute character seems to demand that such vindication cannot be permanently withheld, and since it is not given in this life, will be given hereafter. But to speak of the moral law surviving death, and no persons surviving, is absurd, for such law exists only for, and has meaning only for, persons. Finally, the moral argument gains its authority from something more than itself. Where there is a law we believe there must be a lawgiver, and agree with Abraham, 'Shall not the Judge of all the earth do right?'

(3) *Argument of Personal Consciousness.* Our primary and fundamental reality is our own consciousness. 'Cogito ergo sum.' Can we really conceive of its annihilation? Technically, we certainly cannot think of extinction of thought, even if we could conceive of extinction of our own consciousness. The average man has no difficulty in imagining the material world going on exactly the same with all life removed from it. But a very little philosophy will convince him that all he knows is known through his mind, and to imagine that objects can continue as minds know them when there are no minds, is a plain contradiction. On the same grounds, the annihilation of all consciousness is inconceivable in the literal sense of the term 'inconceivable,' for there must still be consciousness left to conceive the annihilation of consciousness. This argument is one that best bases itself on idealism. But in any case, there is not the slightest reason for immortalizing energy or atoms and annihilating consciousness. Our one certainty is thought. The science of to-day may be gone to-morrow. We have already seen matter, which seemed so real, disappear into a complicated set of mathematical equations, but consciousness survives—the greatest of realities. This is so much reason for holding that it

The Philosophical Approach to Religion

survives the death it alone can anticipate. Certainly, we have no analogy for thinking that what is can become what is not, something evaporating into nothing. There is therefore the strongest possible ground for believing consciousness cannot be extinguished by death. At any rate, if so, it would be an outstanding miracle.

The real point, therefore, is not so much whether consciousness survives, as whether personal consciousness does so. It may be admitted that something cannot be nothing, but urged that it can change into something else so different as to be unrecognizable. Yet this is not fatal to the argument. Personality is certainly something; indeed, an outstanding fact in reality, and it is also something unique. For it gives to man an individuality and distinctness which nothing else possesses. Apparently, even electrons have no permanent identity. If, then, we apply the argument again, personality is, and therefore cannot conceivably be imagined as becoming what is not. But because it is unique and possesses individuality which nothing else possesses, we may refuse to accept analogy drawn from material things, which suggests that personality can be so changed that it becomes unrecognizable, even though surviving.

Further objection urged against this argument is that of man's insignificance in the cosmos. But all this is to treat what James called the 'block universe' as a kind of brute fact, self-existent. Actually, however, space and time which make the vastness of the universe belong not to it, but to human experience. Moreover, it is a sign of man's greatness that his intellect has discovered the very facts about the universe supposed to belittle him. It is natural for man to experience a sense of awe when he gazes at the starry heaven above. Yet the true meaning of greatness is not found in the stars, which know not their own existence, but in the mind of man, who 'thinks God's thoughts after him.'

(4) *Argument from Desire.* May we take our capacity for conceiving immortality and our desire for it as indications that it exists for us? This argument has been ridiculed, e.g. by saying that because we desire a dinner there must be a dinner for us! But this is a little too clever. The point is, if there were no such thing as food, there would be no such thing as hunger, and vice-versa. At any rate, in the physical world there is no

Immortality

desire that is not in some way answered by the environment, and the argument from the desire for immortality can be met only by maintaining that whereas physical desires are honoured, spiritual desires correspond to nothing. In view of the psychological relation between feeling and thought, this is somewhat precarious. Moreover, philosophy has always been ready to agree that the human mind can attain truth. But if we ask why it should think so, the only possible answer is because it feels itself capable of entertaining truth, and desires to attain it, which is precisely the argument for immortality. It follows that if we are to believe ourselves capable of attaining truth but not immortality, we are assuming that our intellectual powers are the sole guide to what is real, whilst our affective and volitional nature has no such significance. This type of intellectualism was possible for the Greeks, but it can no longer be maintained in view of the functional character of reason. It is impossible to prove that a universe which mocks our moral judgements and has no relation to our feelings and desires, can be a universe which will respond to our intellectual attempts to comprehend it.

Moreover, we may also urge that our sense of the good indicates the character of the ground of our being, and that value and actuality cannot be entirely divorced. In fine, we do not create ourselves or our ideals or our hopes of the hereafter. Our mental life, no less than our physical life, must be traced back to the source of our being, and those who maintain that such a desire has no significance, must maintain that the Power that made us has allowed us to think, hope and expect a future which does not exist for us, which is hardly rational, let alone moral. But we are rational and moral, and it is difficult to believe we are superior to the source of our being.

(5) *Argument from Values*. Values, like truth, beauty and goodness, exist only for mind, and for an idealist, at any rate, point to the supreme mind in which they are completely realized. God therefore represents not only the supreme value, but the ground of all values, and if, as was suggested in Chapter III, all religions explicitly or implicitly testify God is love, then men are values to God's love. We believe our own values are objective, and we can hardly think that what is of value to God can be allowed to perish. We think our highest ideals show us the nature of reality, and if so, our ideal of life

triumphant over death is not a subjective notion, but represents what God our maker has allowed us to think, and we cannot believe that He has misled us. As a last resort, therefore, belief in immortality is grounded on the nature of God rather than on the nature of men, on God's honour rather than on man's importance, and on the deep conviction that we who cherish our values and preserve them, are not more careful of value than God, who will surely let none of His values perish out of His hands.

The Nature of Immortality

(1) *Is it Universal?* Immortality is not 'a talismanic gift conferred indiscriminately on every being born of human shape' (Pringle-Pattison, *Idea of Immortality*, p. 195). Personality is made, not given, and souls grow and are not fixed. Possibly, therefore, a self with no moral unity is not a true and enduring self, and may not be able to resist the disintegration of death. Such souls have lived, and yet, as Dante says, 'never were alive'. Milton invented a special Limbo for them, called the Paradise of Fools, the home of 'embryos and idiots, eremites and friars, white, black and grey, with all their trumperies'. He believed in natural immortality, and did not wish to consign all these to hell. Others deny natural immortality and say that what in a true sense has never been, cannot continue to be. The theological doctrine of conditional immortality associated with Edward White and others, is on similar lines, and affords a check to an easy universalism, as the one is certainly as thinkable as the other.

The question of immortality of the animals also occurs here, and while one may believe that nothing which is can perish, and that life therefore goes on, it may be that unless life develops into an individual expression sufficient to survive its separation from the body, it may drop back to the common stock of life, mass rather than individual survival. Thus the animal's spirit may finally dissolve into 'souldust' and lose its individuality as does the body, but it is possible that the higher animals have a more individual survival.

(2) *Character of After-Life.* It seems reasonable to assume that this life and the next are continuous, and we resume existence hereafter at the point where we have left off here. If so, this

Immortality

life is preparatory to the other, and some relation must surely exist between the character of the training and the end for which we are trained. This seems to make ridiculous the notion that the struggle of this life closes with eternal inactivity in heaven. It suggests that we are trained to fight the good fight here and to seek the highest values that we may continue to seek them hereafter. Here we know them only by contrast with their opposites, as we know light by contrast with darkness, yet light is a positive thing physically, and darkness is simply its absence. There would still be light if there were no darkness. Similarly beauty, truth and goodness would exist were there no error, ugliness and sin, and in their positive aspect would exhibit qualities that we who have known them only in their contrast aspect, cannot realize. It seems, therefore, the best conception of the after-life we can attain is that of activity in quest for, and progressive attainment of, the positive aspect and fulness of eternal values which now we see in a glass enigmatically, but then face to face.

INDEX OF PROPER NAMES

Abraham, 181
Achan, 34
Aenesidemus, 54
Agassiz, 71
Agrippa, 54
Aken-Haten, 156
Aladdin, 179
Alexander, S., 89, 90, 92, 159
Anaxagoras, 71
Anselm, 65, 66, 68, 78, 80, 168
Aquinas, 157, 163, 168
Arcesilaus, 54
Argyll, Duke of, 74
Aristotle, 13, 38, 48, 60, 67, 68, 71, 89, 91, 94, 106, 133, 136, 157, 167
Arnold, Matthew, 21
Aubrey, 62
Augustine, 61-3, 119, 157

Bacon, Roger, 26, 164
Balfour, 53, 105
Barth, 155, 161
Bentham, 133, 134
Bergson, 77, 91, 106, 123, 124, 129
Berkeley, 48, 106, 107, 108, 110, 115
Booth, William, 138
Bosanquet, 115
Bradlaugh, 56
Bradley, F. H., 54, 67, 77, 82, 98, 115, 148, 160
Broad, C. D., 177
Bruno, 147
Büchner, 103
Butler, 35, 64, 80, 134, 140, 152, 153, 154

Caesar, 24, 91, 150
Caird, John, 67, 119, 123
Carneades, 54
Clarke, Samuel, 151
Collins, Anthony, 152
Comte, 56
Confucius, 118, 138
Copernicus, 26
Crawley, A. E., 22
Croce, 14, 29

Dalton, 104
Dante, 184
Darwin, 13, 15, 25, 26, 42, 52, 57, 72, 73, 74, 75, 103, 137, 138, 171
Democritus, 103
Descartes, 41, 43, 62, 68, 95, 106, 111
Dewey, John, 47
Driesch, 74
Durkheim, 15, 21, 22, 23, 80

Eddington, 113, 125
Edwards, Jonathan, 31, 119, 123
Einstein, 58, 84
Emerson, 147
Epicurus, 103
Erigena, 147, 148, 168

Faraday, 26
Ferrier, 38
Fitzgerald and Lorenz, 28
Flint, 103, 148
Frazer, Sir James, 19, 21, 22, 24

Galileo, 26
Galsworthy, 88
Gaunilo, 66
Gladstone, 164
Gotama Buddha, 59, 157
Gray, Asa, 73
Green, T. H., 46, 137, 142, 158
Grossetête, 26
Gwatkin, 82

Haeckel, 97, 99, 104, 114, 149
Hamilton, Sir William, 55, 57
Harnack, 62
Harrison, Frederic, 56
Hegel, 14, 20, 29, 63, 66, 67, 97, 101, 102, 137, 147
Heisenberg, 125
Helmholtz, 73
Herbart, 132
Herbert, Lord of Cherbury, 151, 163
Hermann, M., 29
Hobbes, Thomas, 14, 62, 103, 119, 134
Holyoake, G. J., 56
Homer, 119, 146
Howerth, Ira G., 24
Howison, 102
Hudson, W. H., 171
Hume, 14, 45, 46, 48, 55, 63, 64, 71, 110, 153, 154
Huxley, 55, 73, 164, 170, 178

Illingworth, 127

Jacobi, 161
James, William, 22, 46, 47, 48, 57, 69, 101, 102, 123, 146, 178, 179, 182
Jeans, Sir James, 113, 125, 158
Jerome, 168
Jevons, 145
Joachim, H., 48
Johnson, Dr., 123
Justinian, 61

Index of Proper Names

Kant, 14, 20, 29, 36, 39, 41, 43, 47, 55, 64, 65, 66, 70, 72, 78, 79, 80, 95, 114, 115, 130, 137, 164, 165, 176, 178, 179
Keith, Sir Arthur, 71
Kelvin, 104
Kepler, 26

La Mettrie, 103
Lang, Andrew, 156
Lao-Tse, 138
Lecky, 147
Leibniz, 42, 43, 63, 99, 100, 102, 106, 169
Leland, 151, 152
Lewes, G.H., 38, 45
Locke, 43, 45, 48, 70, 95, 108, 151
Lotze, 39, 66, 70, 87, 97, 108, 133, 169
Lucretius, 13
Lyell, 26

McTaggart, J. E., 21, 40, 67, 81, 101, 102, 115
Macmurray, John, 39
McDougall, 112
Mansel, Dean, 56, 164
Marett, 16
Martineau, Harriet, 178
Martineau, James, 80, 140, 161
Mather, 105
Mencius, 103
Menzies, 23
Michelson and Morley, 28
Mill, J. S., 45, 114, 134, 135
Millikan, 158
Milton, 184
Moore, G. E., 45, 140
Moses, 177
Muhammad, 131, 165
Myers, F. W. H., 20

Newton, 26, 38, 160
Nicholas of Autrecourt, 106
Nietzsche, 14, 137, 139

Origen, 157, 168
Otto, 161

Paley, 72, 73, 134, 160, 178
Papini, 48
Parmenides, 106, 147
Pascal, 119
Paul, St., 62, 146, 172
Perpetua, 127
Petronius, 13, 14
Picton, Allanson, 148, 149
Pierce, Charles Sanders, 47
Plato, 27, 32, 38, 43, 54, 59, 60, 61, 67, 71, 94, 106, 131, 146, 175, 176, 178

Plotinus, 61, 94, 98, 149
Priestley, 135
Prince, Morton, 97
Pringle-Pattison, 101, 168, 184
Pyrrho of Elis, 41, 53
Pythagoras, 26, 38, 71, 105, 176

Rashdall, Dean, 70, 80, 81, 109, 111
Rasmussen, 24
Rawdon, Lord, 153
Rousseau, 119, 138, 152
Ruskin, 118
Russell, Bertrand, 76, 104, 124

Samuel, 24
Santayana, 106
Schiller, Dr. F. C. S., 44, 47
Schleiermacher, 14, 176
Schopenhauer, 97, 147, 150
Sextus Empiricus, 54
Shelley, 32, 147
Sidgwick, 133, 134, 135
Smith, N. Kemp, 75
Socrates, 48
Solomon, 31, 145
Spencer, Herbert, 15, 21, 38, 45, 55, 115, 138
Spinoza, 20, 43, 62, 95, 97, 102, 114, 147, 148, 176
St. Francis, 109
Streeter, 127

Tennyson, 150
Tertullian, 61, 83, 168
Tindal, Matthew, 152, 153
Toland, 152
Tucker, Abraham, 134
Tylor, Sir E. B., 15

Ussher, 26

Vaihinger, 41
Voltaire, 152
Von Hartmann, 150
Von Holbach, 103

Wallace, 171
Ward James, 76, 85, 95, 102, 124, 179
Wesley, John, 31, 153, 154
Westermarck, 16, 35, 141
White, Edward, 184
Whitehead, A. N., 21, 74, 89, 90, 91, 92, 105, 159
Wolff, 95, 97
Wordsworth, 52, 76

Xenophanes, 147

Zeno, 54
Zoroaster, 156

www.ingramcontent.com/pod-product-compliance
Lightning Source LLC
Chambersburg PA
CBHW051929160426
43198CB00012B/2089